"A Pretty Girl Is Like a Melody"
and Other Favorite Song Hits
1918–1919

Edited by
DAVID A. JASEN

DOVER PUBLICATIONS, INC.
Mineola, New York

DOVER MUSICAL ARCHIVES

Bibliographical Note

"A Pretty Girl Is Like a Melody" and Other Favorite Song Hits, 1918–1919 is a new work, first published by Dover Publications, Inc., in 1997. It consists of unabridged, unaltered republications of the sheet music of 40 popular songs (original publishers and dates of publication are indicated in the Contents), as well as a new Introduction and Alphabetical List of Songwriters and Lyricists.

International Standard Book Number: 0-486-29421-8

Manufactured in the United States of America
Dover Publications, Inc., 31 East 2nd Street, Mineola, N.Y. 11501

Introduction

This collection of popular songs continues Dover's ongoing series linking us to our musical past in what we sang, hummed and whistled through this century. As we look back, it is good to be reminded of this early popular literature—what those covers and music sheets looked like, and how the songs sounded in their original versions. Yet, this collection is like none of the others in our series, for it brings together Tin Pan Alley's pioneers as well as its then-newcomers, many destined for fame as the creators of future standards.

The names of these composers and lyricists capsulize the best of the Alley—from musical-theater stalwarts Victor Herbert and Robert B. Smith to later champs Harry Tierney and Joseph McCarthy. The pop song is represented by veterans Ernest R. Ball, Jean Schwartz and Fred Fisher, and by newcomers Richard Whiting, Pete Wendling, Buddy De Sylva and Lew Brown, among many others. Hit writers of the period—people like Bert Kalmar, Joe Young and Sam Lewis—are welcomed by long-time veterans Irving Berlin, Gus Kahn, Albert Van Tilzer and their many contemporaries.

The years 1918–19 were a time of record breakers. The musical *Irene*—with its hit song "Alice Blue Gown"—ran for an astonishing 675 performances, a record unmatched for another 18 years. "Beautiful Ohio" and "Till We Meet Again" vied for selling the most sheets of any song in 1918—a record five million copies each! ("Beautiful Ohio" became the biggest seller in Shapiro, Bernstein's publishing history.) "Somebody Stole My Gal," a resounding flop on arrival, wound up a million-copy hit, and an all-time standard, following later recordings by the Original Memphis Five and Bix Beiderbecke and His Gang.

While more songs were written about World War I than any other American war, few were spectacularly successful. Sergeant Irving Berlin scored with his autobiographical "Oh, How I Hate to Get Up in the Morning," while Walter Donaldson—entertaining the troops at the same Camp Upton where Berlin was stationed—asked the farsighted question "How 'Ya Gonna Keep 'em Down on the Farm (After They've Seen Paree)?"

Pete Wendling's "Oh! What a Pal Was Mary" joined the million-seller sensations as did George Gershwin's "Swanee" (thanks to pal Al Jolson) and Creamer and Layton's "After You've Gone" (thanks to Sophie Tucker). And time has transformed Berlin's evergreen "A Pretty Girl Is Like a Melody" from a Ziegfeld Follies theme song to a standard for *all* time—and for fashion shows yet to come!

The great variety of hit songs in this special collection, and the stability of their place in our national musical literature, point up the enduring success of the Alley and its domination of a significant corner of our popular culture. Today's remembrance of those long-ago sounds, especially in the face of changing musical taste, is a twofold tribute: we take pleasure in their unfading freshness as we honor their place in our history.

David A. Jasen

Contents

The songs are arranged in alphabetical order, using their titles as printed either on the first page of music of the original sheets or else on the cover, and not counting "A" or "The" at the beginning of the title. The publishers given here (abbreviated "Pub.") are those indicated on the covers of the specific first or early editions being reprinted. The years are those of copyright.

Reference works cited are APS: *American Popular Songs*, David Ewen, ed.: Random House, N.Y., 1966; GST: *The Great Song Thesaurus* by Roger Lax & Frederick Smith: Oxford University Press, N.Y., 2nd ed., 1989; HPMA: *A History of Popular Music in America* by Sigmund Spaeth: Random House, N.Y., 1948; and VMC: *Variety Music Cavalcade* by Julius Mattfeld: Prentice-Hall, Inc., N.J., 3rd ed., 1971.

Alphabetical List
of Songwriters and Lyricists

Milton Ager (1893–1979): composer, publisher; major collaboration with lyricist Jack Yellen; hits: "Ain't She Sweet," "Happy Days Are Here Again," "I'm Nobody's Baby," "Hard-Hearted Hannah," "I Wonder What's Become of Sally."

Ernest R. Ball (1878–1927): composer; his sentimental favorites include Tin Pan Alley's legendary Irish ballads "When Irish Eyes Are Smiling," "A Little Bit of Heaven (And They Called It Ireland)," "Mother Machree" (a staple in the concert repertoire of tenor John McCormack) and "Goodbye, Good Luck, God Bless You"; his million-seller "Love Me and the World Is Mine" led to a lucrative 20-year contract with Witmark, a Tin Pan Alley "first" for a long-term agreement between composer and publisher; the 1944 film *When Irish Eyes Are Smiling* was Ball's screen biography.

Irving Berlin (1888–1989): Russian-born composer, lyricist, music publisher, theater owner; author of some 1500 songs between 1907 and 1966, for Tin Pan Alley, 19 stage shows and 18 motion pictures; a major influential figure of American entertainment, he is especially remembered for such standards as "God Bless America," "Easter Parade," "White Christmas," for the Broadway shows *Annie Get Your Gun* and *Call Me Madam*, and for such films as *Top Hat* and *Holiday Inn*.

Felix Bernard (1897–1944): composer; while his "Twenty-one Dolls a Day Once a Month" is lost in pop-music history, Bernard's "Winter Wonderland" became a Yuletide classic, selling a million copies of the Andrews Sisters' 1950 recording.

Johnny S. Black: composer, lyricist; essentially a two-hit songwriter, his music for "Dardanella" (co-written with Felix Bernard) was joined a decade later by his own words and music for "Paper Doll" (unpublished until 1942!).

Walter Blaufuss (1883–1945): composer; songs: "My Isle of Golden Dreams," "Some Time When Lights Are Low," "Swanee Ripples Rag."

James Alexander Brennan (1885–1956): composer (incorrectly listed as "Joseph" in standard references); nostalgic songs include "In the Little Red Schoolhouse," "Down at the Old Swimming Hole," "Barefoot Days."

J. Keirn Brennan (1873–1948): lyricist; songs: "Ireland Is Ireland to Me," "Empty Saddles" (introduced by Bing Crosby in the film *Rhythm on the Range*), "My Bird of Paradise" and, with composer Ernest R. Ball, the popular "A Little Bit of Heaven (And They Called It Ireland)."

Monty C. Brice: lyricist; his "The Daughter of Rosie O'Grady," written with Walter Donaldson, became the young Pat Rooney's song-and-dance trademark.

Lew Brown (1893–1958): lyricist, publisher (with lyricist Bud De Sylva and composer Ray Henderson); numerous hits include "Lucky in Love," "You're the Cream in My Coffee," "Button Up Your Overcoat," "Sunny Side Up," "That Old Feeling," "Don't Sit Under the Apple Tree (with Anyone Else But Me)"—a favorite of G.I.s in World War II—"The Best Things in Life Are Free" (the title of the 1956 film biography of De Sylva, Brown and Henderson) and "The Birth of the Blues," selected by ASCAP in 1963 as one of the 16 songs of its all-time Hit Parade.

Alfred Bryan (1871–1958?): lyricist for films, Broadway; wrote "Peg o' My Heart," "Come, Josephine, in My Flying Machine," "I Didn't Raise My Boy to Be a Soldier," "The Country Cousin," "Oui, Oui, Marie," "Ireland Must Be Heaven"; shows include *Shubert Gaieties of 1919*, *The Midnight Rounders*.

James J. Caddigan (1879–1952): lyricist (incorrectly listed as "Caddingan" in standard references); wrote "We're All Going Calling on the Kaiser" (with James A. Brennan), "Little French Mother, Goodbye."

Irving Caesar (1895–   ): lyricist, publisher; hit songs: "Animal Crackers in My Soup" (introduced by Shirley Temple), "Is It True What They Say about Dixie?" and "Umbriago," the latter written with and for Jimmy Durante; Caesar's "Tea for Two" was selected by ASCAP in 1963 as one of the 16 songs of its all-time Hit Parade.

J. Will Callahan (1874–1946): lyricist, author; wrote many songs (including "When I Came Home to You," "The Flag We Love"), but only "Smiles" was a solid hit.

Bob Carleton (1896–1956): composer; songs: "Teasin'," "Where the Blues Were Born in New Orleans."

Harry Carroll (1892–1962): composer; wrote "On the Mississippi" (his first song hit), "Trail of the Lonesome Pine," "By the Beautiful Sea," "Down in Bom-Bombay," "There's a Girl in the Heart of Maryland."

Grant Clarke (1891–1931): lyricist; songs include "Ragtime Cowboy Joe," "Second-Hand Rose," "Am I Blue?," "Weary River."

Leslie Cooke: lyricist of "Love Sends a Little Gift of Roses." *(No further information is available.)*

Eddie Cox: lyricist, with Bert Kalmar, of "You Said It!" *(No further information is available.)*

Henry Creamer (1879–1930): lyricist; other hits (with composer John Turner Layton) include "'Way Down Yonder in New Orleans," "Dear Old Southland," "Sweet Emalina, My Gal," "If I Could Be With You One Hour Tonight."

Bud (Buddy) De Sylva (1895–1950): lyricist, composer, publishing partner of Lew Brown and Ray Henderson; a major figure of the Jolson-Cantor era, he wrote "If You Knew Susie," "Alabamy Bound," "When Day Is Done," "Broken Hearted," "The Varsity Drag," "You're the Cream in My Coffee," "Sunny Side Up," "Button Up Your Overcoat."

Walter Donaldson (1891–1947): composer, lyricist, publisher; major hits: "My Blue Heaven," "(What Can I Say, Dear) After I Say I'm Sorry," "Carolina in the Morning," "Makin' Whoopee," "Love Me or Leave Me," "My Baby Just Cares for Me," "Little White Lies," "My Buddy," "You're Driving Me Crazy," "Yes, Sir, That's My Baby."

Mary Earl (1861–1932): one of several pseudonyms (some feminine) of the prolific composer Robert A. Keiser; according to HPMA, he also wrote under the names Vivian Grey ("Anona"), Ed Haley ("The Fountain in the Park" ["While Strolling through the Park One Day"]), Bob (Robert A.) King ("Beyond the Gates of Paradise"), Kathleen A. Roberts ("Apple Blossoms"), R. A. Wilson ("Peep-Boo") and Mrs. Ravenhall (no song titles given); other hits include "(I Scream, You Scream, We All Scream for) Ice Cream," "I Ain't Nobody's Darling," "Why Did I Kiss That Girl?"

Raymond B. Egan (1890–1952): lyricist; songs include "I Never Knew," "There Ain't No Maybe in My Baby's Eyes," "And They Called It Dixieland."

Fred Fisher (originally **Fischer**) (1875–1942): composer, lyricist, publisher; one of the era's most prolific, successful collaborators; hits include "Peg o' My Heart," "Chicago," "Come Josephine in My Flying Machine," "They Go Wild, Simply Wild, Over Me," "Your Feet's Too Big" (a Fats Waller specialty), "I Found a Rose in the Devil's Garden" and "Who Paid the Rent for Mrs. Rip Van Winkle?"; actor S. Z. "Cuddles" Sakall played Fisher in his 1949 film biography, *Oh, You Beautiful Doll* (*not*, for the record, a Fisher tune!).

Byron Gay (1886–1945): composer, lyricist; songs: "Little Ford Rambled Right Along," "Horses" (with Richard A. Whiting), "Fate," "Sand Dunes" and "The Vamp," inspired by silent-screen actress Theda Bara.

George Gershwin (1898–1937): composer, pianist; one of the all-time great composers for the American musical stage, his Broadway shows include *Lady, Be Good, Tip-toes, Oh, Kay!, Funny Face, Strike Up the Band, Of Thee I Sing, Girl Crazy*; countless hit songs written with his brother, lyricist Ira Gershwin, include "Bidin' My Time," "Fascinating Rhythm," "But Not for Me," "The Man I Love," "Someone to Watch Over Me," "I Got Rhythm," "Embraceable You," "A Foggy Day"; his *Rhapsody in Blue*, Piano Concerto in F and "folk opera" *Porgy and Bess* broke new ground—the latter adding such modern classics as "Summertime," "I Got Plenty o' Nuthin'," "Bess, You Is My Woman Now" and "It Ain't Necessarily So."

Victor Herbert (1859–1924): composer, bandmaster, founder/charter member of ASCAP; legendary figure in American musical theater; shows and operettas include *Babes in Toyland, Mlle. Modiste, The Red Mill, Naughty Marietta, Sweethearts*; among his all-time classics: "Ah! Sweet Mystery of Life," "Every Day is Ladies' Day with Me," "Gypsy Love Song," "I'm Falling in Love with Some One," "Italian Street Song," "March of the Toys," "Romany Life," "The Streets of New York," "Toyland"; between 1893–1900, Herbert led the famous Gilmore band following its founder's death.

Art Hickman (1886–1930): composer, bandleader; wrote "June Moon," "Hold Me" (introduced in the *Ziegfeld Follies of 1920*) and "You and I" (not to be confused with Meredith Willson's 1941 hit of the same name, recorded by Glenn Miller, which became the signature music for the Maxwell House radio program).

Arnold Johnson (1893–1975): composer, bandleader; PeeWee Hunt's hit 1953 recording of "O" sold over a million copies; other hits include "Sweetheart" (*not* the Sigmund Romberg classic), "Tear Drops" and "Goodbye Blues."

Al Jolson (born Asa Yoelson) (1886–1950): singer-entertainer, lyricist, composer; unique, extraordinarily popular personality of vaudeville, minstrel shows, Broadway, films; starred in *The Jazz Singer*, the first commercial feature film with songs and some dialogue spelling the end of the silent-film era; other films include *The Singing Fool, Say It with Songs, Mammy, Hallelujah, I'm a Bum* and *The Jolson Story* (soundtrack only); many song hits include: "The Anniversary Song," "Back in Your Own Back Yard," "California, Here I Come," "Me and My Shadow" (popularized by bandleader Ted Lewis), "Bagdad," "There's a Rainbow 'Round My Shoulder" (a Jolson specialty) and "Sonny Boy" (a million-record seller); for his popular "Avalon," Jolson was successfully sued for copyright infringement by G. Ricordi, publisher of Puccini's opera *Tosca*.

Gustave (Gus) Kahn (1886–1941): lyricist; highlights of his many legendary successes include "Side by Side," "I'll See You in My Dreams," "The Carioca," "Yes, Sir, That's My Baby," "It Had to Be You," "Toot, Toot, Tootsie, Goodbye," "Pretty Baby," "Flying Down to Rio," "San Francisco."

Bert Kalmar (1884–1947): lyricist, publisher; songs by the successful team of Kalmar and Harry Ruby include "I Wanna Be Loved by You," "A Kiss to Build a Dream On," "She's Funny That Way," "Who's Sorry Now?" and "Watching the Clouds Roll By"; the hit "Three Little Words" became the title song of the team's 1950 film biography, starring Fred Astaire and Red Skelton.

John William Kellette and **Jaan Kenbrovin**: pen names for **James Kendis** (1883–1946), **James Brockman** (1886–1967) and **Nat Vincent** (1889–1979); "I'm Forever Blowing Bubbles" is the only time these three veteran songwriters used these pseudonyms.

John Turner Layton (1894–1978): composer, pianist; memorable songs include "Strut Miss Lizzie," " 'Way Down Yonder in New Orleans."

Edgar Leslie (1885–1976): lyricist; major collaborator with Irving Berlin, Harry Warren, others; hits include "For Me and My Gal," "Moon Over Miami," "Among My Souvenirs," "It Looks Like Rain in Cherry Blossom Lane" and the popular World War I song "America, I Love You."

Sam M. Lewis (1885–1959): lyricist, charter member of ASCAP; with chief lyrics collaborator Joe Young wrote "My Mammy" (Al Jolson's signature song), "Dinah," "In a Little Spanish Town," "Just Friends," "I Believe in Miracles," "For All We Know"; many other standards (see Joe Young's credits).

Robert Lloyd: composer, lyricist; Lloyd is identified solely as an "Army Song Leader." *(No further information is available.)*

Eugene Lockhart (died 1957): actor, lyricist, stage director; shortening his name to Gene, Lockhart became one of Hollywood's most distinguished character actors (daughter June Lockhart starred on stage and screen, as well); wrote "A Modest Little Thing," "Balm," "Swish," "The Way to Your Heart," "It's Home to Me," "Love's Riddle."

Ballard Macdonald (1882–1935): lyricist; charter member of ASCAP; important songs include "Parade of the Wooden Soldiers," "The Trail of the Lonesome Pine," "Clap Hands, Here Comes Charlie," "Somebody Loves Me."

Joseph McCarthy (1885–1943): lyricist; hits include "They Go Wild, Simply Wild, Over Me," "Rio Rita," "The Kinkajou," "Ireland Must Be Heaven for My Mother Came from There"; his classic "You Made Me Love You" was introduced by Al Jolson.

George W. Meyer (1884–1947): composer, charter member of ASCAP; hits: "For Me and My Gal," "Sittin' in a Corner," "I'm a Little Blackbird Looking for a Bluebird," "Mandy, Make Up Your Mind," "I Believe in Miracles."

Geoffrey O'Hara (1882–1967): composer, lyricist; "K-K-K-Katy" was his only hit song; O'Hara is identified in the publication as an "Army Song Leader" as well as "Composer of 'Over Yonder Where The Lilies Grow,' etc."

John Openshaw: composer of "Love Sends a Little Gift of Roses." *(No further information is available.)*

Arthur A. Penn (1875–1941): composer, lyricist; another one-hit songwriter ("Smilin' Through").

Camille Robert: composer of "Madelon." *(No further information is available.)*

Lee S. Roberts (1884–1949): composer, pianist; best known as music director and performer for *QRS Piano Rolls*; the hit "Smiles" was his sole success, selling over three million copies of sheet music despite having been rejected by every major Tin Pan Alley publisher.

Henry W. Santley (1890–1934): composer, publisher; songs: "Will You Remember Me?," "I'll Find a Way to Forget You," "What Good is Good Morning?"

Jean Schwartz (1878–1956): composer; wrote such diverse hits as "Rip van Winkle Was a Lucky Man," "Bedelia," "Chinatown, My Chinatown," "Hello Central, Give Me No Man's Land" and "Rock-a-Bye Your Baby with a Dixie Melody" (an Al Jolson highlight).

Ernest J. Seitz: Canadian concert pianist, conductor, teacher. *(No further information is available.)*

Robert Bache Smith (1875–1951): lyricist; collaborated with Victor Herbert, Reginald de Koven; wrote "Jeanette and Her Little Wooden Shoes," "Sweethearts" (with Herbert), "The Little Girl in Blue," "Come Down, Ma Evenin' Star" (a sentimental Lillian Russell specialty).

Harry Tierney (1890–1965): composer; songs include "M-i-s-s-i-s-s-i-p-p-i," "Irene," "Rio Rita," "The Kinkajou," "The Rangers' Song," "If You Can't Get a Girl in the Summertime."

Egbert Van Alstyne (1882–1951): composer, lyricist; songs: "In the Shade of the Old Apple Tree," "San Antonio," "Pretty Baby," "Memories," "Good Night, Ladies," "Beautiful Love" and his first hit song, "Navajo" (see remarks under Harry H. Williams).

Albert Von Tilzer (born Albert Gumm) (1878–1956): composer, lyricist, publisher; hits include "Put Your Arms Around Me, Honey," "I'll Be with You in Apple Blossom Time," "Chili Bean," "Dapper Dan (the Sheik of Alabam')," "Smarty," "Honey Boy" (a tribute to the celebrated minstrel George "Honey Boy" Evans) and "Take Me Out to the Ball Game," the unofficial anthem of America's national pastime.

Oliver George Wallace (1887–1963): composer; wrote film scores for Disney's *Dumbo* (Academy Award, 1941), *Cinderella*, *Alice in Wonderland*; as G. Oliver Wallace, he is credited as composer/lyricist for the World War II comedy song "Der Fuehrer's Face," lampooning Hitler, written for the Donald Duck animated cartoon of the same title (popularized in a wacky arrangement by Spike Jones and His City Slickers, the song sold over 1.5 million records).

Harold Taylor Weeks (1893–1922): composer, lyricist; songs include "Cairo," "Tropical Moonlight."

Pete Wendling (1888–1974): composer, pianist; his pseudo-Hawaiian "Yacka Hula Hickey Dula" heads a list of songs including "Take Me to the Land of Jazz," "Red Lips, Kiss My Blues Away," "There's Danger in Your Eyes, Cherie" (introduced by Harry Richman), "I Believe in Miracles" and "On the Street of Regret."

Richard A. Whiting (1891–1938): one of the era's most successful composers, his string of hits include "Japanese Sandman," "Sleepy Time Gal," "Breezin' Along with the Breeze," "Louise" (introduced by Maurice Chevalier in his American screen debut), "Beyond the Blue Horizon," "You're an Old Smoothie," "On the Good Ship Lollypop" (made famous by Shirley Temple), "Hooray for Hollywood" (Tinsel Town's popular anthem), "Ain't We Got Fun?" and "Too Marvelous for Words"—the song that launched daughter Margaret Whiting's big-band singing career.

Harry H. Williams (1879–1922): lyricist, publisher; with composer Neil Moret wrote "Mickey (Pretty Mickey)," the first theme song written to exploit a motion picture (Mabel Normand's 1918 silent film *Mickey*); with composer Egbert Van Alstyne wrote the 1903 hit "Navajo," the first successful popular song about the American Indian (touching off a Tin Pan Alley vogue); their follow-up hits included "San Antonio" and especially "In the Shade of the Old Apple Tree."

Leo Wood (1882–1929): composer, lyricist; besides "Somebody Stole My Gal" (his biggest hit), wrote "Runnin' Wild," "Honest and Truly," "Cherie."

Joe Young (1889–1939): lyricist, charter member of ASCAP; with chief lyricist-collaborator Sam M. Lewis wrote such hits as "How 'Ya Gonna Keep 'em Down on the Farm," "Five Foot Two, Eyes of Blue," "I'm Sitting on Top of the World" (popularized by Al Jolson) and "Where Did Robinson Crusoe Go with Friday on Saturday Night?"; (for other titles, see Sam M. Lewis' credits).

AFTER YOU'VE GONE
BY
CREAMER & LAYTON
5
BROADWAY MUSIC CORPORATION
WILL VON TILZER PRESIDENT
145 WEST 45TH ST, NEW YORK

After You've Gone

By
CREAMER & LAYTON

Now won't you list-en hon-ey while I say___ How could you tell me that you're going a - way
Don't you re-mem-ber how you used to say___ You'd al ways love me in the same old way

Don't say that we must part___ Don't break your ba - by's heart___
And now its ver - y strange That you should ev - er change

You know I've loved you for these man - y years Loved you night and day___
Per-haps some oth - er sweet-ie's won your heart Temp-ted you a - way___

Oh hon - ey ba - by cant you see my tears___ List - en while I say___
But let me warn you tho' we're miles a - part___ You'll re - gret some day___

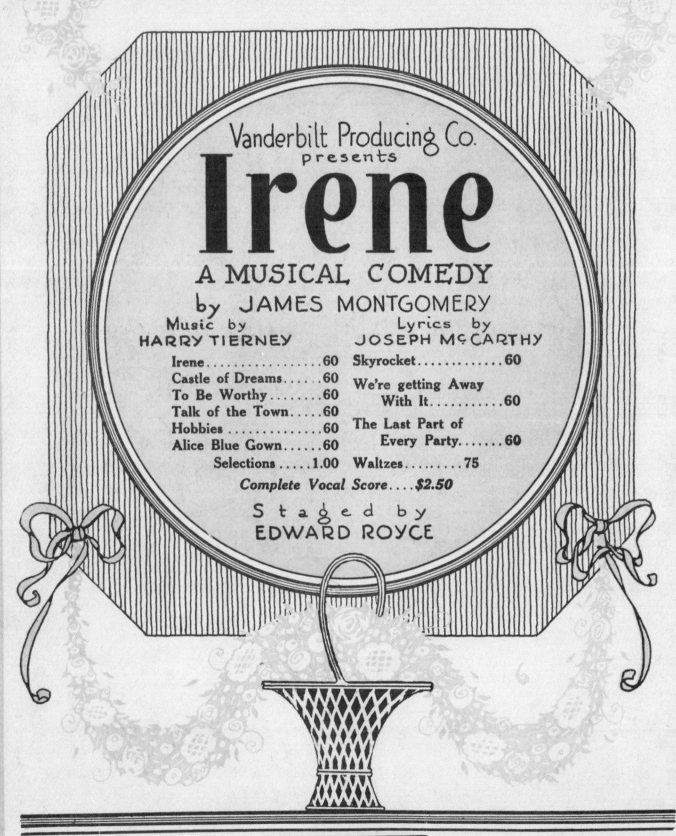

Vanderbilt Producing Co.
presents

Irene

A MUSICAL COMEDY
by JAMES MONTGOMERY

Music by
HARRY TIERNEY

Lyrics by
JOSEPH McCARTHY

Staged by
EDWARD ROYCE

OPERATIC LF EDITION
LEO. FEIST INC. NEW YORK
HERMAN DAREWSKI MUSIC PUBLISHING CO. LONDON, ENG.

Chorus

After you've gone and left me cry-ing After you've gone There's no de-ny-ing, you'll feel blue, You'll feel sad,— You'll miss the best-est pal you've ev-er had— There'll come a time, now don't for-get it, There'll come a time, when you'll re-gret it Oh! Babe, Think what you're do-ing you know my love for you will drive me to ru-in, Af-ter you've gone Af-ter you've gone a-way,— a-way.— way.—

Alice Blue Gown

Lyric by
JOSEPH MC CARTHY

Music by
HARRY TIERNEY

Beautiful Ohio
Song
by
Mary Earl
Lyric by
Ballard Macdonald
INSTRUMENTAL
PIANO SOLO (Waltz)
FULL ORCHESTRA
MILITARY BAND
VOCAL
SONG (Key E flat)
SONG ORCHESTRATION
MALE QUARTETTE
PRICE SIXTY CENTS
PUBLISHED BY
SHAPIRO, BERNSTEIN & CO. INC.
Music Publishers
224 West 47th Street
NEW YORK
THIS NUMBER ON ALL PHONOGRAPH RECORDS AND MUSIC ROLLS

Beautiful Ohio
Song
Adapted from the waltz of the same name

Lyric by
BALLARD MACDONALD

Music by
MARY EARL

Long, long a-go, Some-one I know Had a lit-tle red ca-noe In it room for on-ly two Love found its start, Then in my heart And like a flow-er grew.

Chorus

Drift - ing with the cur-rent down a moon - lit stream While a-bove the Heav - ens in their glo - ry gleam And the stars on high Twin - kle in the sky Seem-ing in a Par - a-dise of love di-vine Dream-ing of a pair of eyes that looked in mine Beau - ti - ful O-

Second Chorus

*When sung as Solo, sing original melody from star

DARDANELLA

BY
FELIX BERNARD
AND
JOHNNY S. BLACK
SONG

WORDS BY
FRED. FISHER

PRICE
SIXTY
CENTS

McCARTHY & FISHER (INC)
MUSIC PUBLISHERS
224 W. 46TH St.   NEW YORK

This
Number is
to be had
on all

PHONOGRAPH
RECORDS AND
MUSIC ROLLS

Ask your Dealer

Dardanella
SONG
Published as an Instrumental Number

Words by
FRED FISHER

Music by
FELIX BERNARD &
JOHNNY S. BLACK

Down _____ be-side the Dar-da-nel-la Bay, Where Or-i-ent-al breezes

When _____ the Turk-ish Sul-tan saw her eyes, Oh he was ta-ken by sur-

play, There lives a lone-some maid, Ar-me-nian. _____

prise, He said I'll buy her for my Ha-rem. _____

By _____ the Dar-da-nelles with glowing eyes, She looks a-cross the seas and
I _____ just told the Sul-tan to be nice, She can't be brought for an-y

sighs, And weaves her love spell so Si - re - nian. _____
price, She said to me she could-n't bear him. _____ *piu mosso*

Soon I shall re-turn to Turk-e - stan, _____
So be - neath the O - ri - en - tal moon, _____

I will ask for her heart and hand: _____
I'll be woo-ing my love real soon: _____

CHORUS

Oh _____ sweet Dar-da-nel - la, I love your ha - rem eyes,

I'm _____ a luck-y fel - low to cap-ture such a prize,

Oh Al - lah knows, my love for you _____ And he tells you to be

true, _____ Dar-da- nel - la, _____ Oh hear my sigh,—

THE DAUGHTER OF ROSIE O'GRADY

NOVELTY WALTZ SONG

WORDS BY
MONTY C. BRICE
MUSIC BY
WALTER DONALDSON
WRITERS OF
"WE'RE COMING BACK TO YOU
WHEN THE FIGHTING DAYS ARE THROUGH"
"YOCK-A-HILO TOWN" Etc.

GLADYS LESLIE
GREATER VITAGRAPH STAR
REPRODUCED BY PERMISSION

M. WITMARK & SONS
NEW YORK CHICAGO PHILADELPHIA BOSTON
SAN FRANCISCO LONDON

50¢
2s/NET

Dedicated to our friend Maud Nugent, author of "SWEET ROSIE O'GRADY"

The Daughter of Rosie O'Grady

Words by
MONTY C. BRICE

Music by
WALTER DONALDSON

Yes-ter-day while out a-walk-in'___ I met a
I'm goin' to ask her to mar-ry___ I won-der

dear lit-tle girl___ Some-how we start-ed a talk-in'___ My brain was all in a
what she will say___ I know that if I should tar-ry___ Some-one will steal her a-

whirl. She said she came from old Kill-ar-ney___ So I start-ed in to quiz___ I
way. I've got the ring to fit her fin-ger___ And if she will name the day___ I'm-

got a sur - prise that op-ened my eyes, For who do you think she is?
a-gine my pride when she is my bride And I hear the neigh - bors say

REFRAIN

She's the daugh-ter of Ro-sie O' Grad - y, A reg-u-lar old fash-ioned girl

She is-n't craz-y for dia - mond rings, Silk-ens and sat-ins and fan-cy things;

She's just a sweet lit-tle lad - y And when you meet her you'll see Why I'm glad I

caught her, the daugh-ter of Ro-sie O' Gra - dy! She's the dy!

Everything is Peaches down in Georgia

Words by Grant Clarke
Music by Milton Ager and Geo. W. Meyer

POPULAR EDITION
LEO. FEIST INC. NEW YORK
HERMAN DAREWSKI MUSIC PUBLISHING CO. LONDON. ENG.

Everything Is Peaches Down In Georgia

Words by
GRANT CLARKE

Music by
MILTON AGER &
GEO. W. MEYER

Down in Georgia there are peaches, Wait-ing for you yes, and each is Sweet____ as an-y
All of Georgia's full of peaches, They're all gorgeous, each one reaches Right____ in-to your

peach____ that you could reach for on a tree.____ Southern beau-ties they are famous
heart____ and makes you part of Georgia too,____ Clingstone peaches cling right to you,

Georgia's where they grow.____ My folks write me, they in-vite me, Don't you want to go?____
Peaches haunt your dream,____ Think of get-ting, al-ways get-ting Peaches in your cream____

CHORUS

Ev'ry thing is peach-es down in Geor - gia,____ What a peach of a clime,____

22

Good Morning, Mr. Zip-Zip-Zip!

Written around a Fort Niagara Fragment
by ROBERT LLOYD,
Army Song Leader

CHORUS (Not fast)

Good morn - ing, Mis-ter Zip-Zip-Zip, With your hair cut just as short as mine, Good

morn - ing, Mis - ter Zip-Zip-Zip, You're sure-ly look-ing fine!

Ash-es to ash-es, and dust to dust, If the Cam-els don't get you, The Fa - ti-mas must, Good

morn - ing, Mis-ter Zip-Zip-Zip, With your hair cut just as short as, your

hair cut just as short as, your hair cut just as short as mine. Good mine.

Hindustan
5
SUCCESSFULLY FEATURED BY
JACK LA FOLLETTE
OLIVER wallace and HAROLD weeks
IRENE EWING

Hindustan.

By OLIVER G. WALLACE
and HAROLD WEEKS

Hin - - - du - stan, _____ where we stopped to rest our tired car - a -
van, _____ Hin - - du - stan, _____ where the paint-ed pea-cock
proud-ly spread his fan, _____ Hin - - du - stan, _____ where the
pur-ple sun-bird flashed a-cross the sand, _____ Hin - - du - stan, _____
___ where I met her and the world be - gan. _____ gan. _____

How 'Ya Gonna Keep 'Em Down On The Farm?

(After They've Seen Paree)

Words by
SAM M. LEWIS
and JOE YOUNG

Music by
WALTER DONALDSON

Chorus

How 'ya gon-na keep 'em, down on the farm, Af-ter they've seen Pa - ree?

How 'ya gon-na keep 'em a - way from Broad-way; Jazz-in' a-'roun', And paint-in' the town?

How 'ya gon-na keep 'em a - way from harm? That's a mys-ter - y;

They'll nev-er want to see a rake or plow, And who the deuce can par-ley-vous a cow?
Im - ag-ine Reu - ben when he meets his pa, He'll kiss his cheek and hol-ler "oo - la - la!"

How 'ya gon-na keep 'em down on the farm, Af-ter they've seen Pa-ree? -ree?

D.S.

D.S.

I'LL SAY SHE DOES

SONG

By BUD De SYLVA
GUS KAHN &
AL JOLSON

Lyrics (Voice line):

I've got a brand new
It was so hard to

sweet - ie __ Bet - ter than the one be - fore __
get her __ She can nev - er get a - way __

Oh! she's got ev - 'ry - thing And a lit - tle bit
Be - cause I'm watch - ing her All the night and all

more
I don't know much a-bout her

day
I've al-ways had her pic - ture

And yet I know a lot

I had it in my mind

'Cause what it takes to

I al-ways knew what

make me love her

kind I want-ed

I want to tell you she's got

And she's ex-act-ly the kind

CHORUS

Does she make ev'-'ry-bo - dy stare

I'll

say she does— Was she hap-py to get— the

ring You bet she was— And can she dance— Can she twist—

Does she do a lot of things I can't re-sist— Does she   I'll say she does—

I'm Always Chasing Rainbows

Harry Carroll & William A. Sheer

present

Oh Look!

A Musical Comedy by
James Montgomery
with
HARRY FOX

Music by
Harry Carroll
Lyrics by
Joseph McCarthy

As Produced at the Vanderbilt Theatre, New York

André C. de Takacs

McCARTHY & FISHER INC.
MUSIC PUBLISHERS
148 W. 45TH St.   NEW YORK

I'm Always Chasing Rainbows

Lyrics by
JOSEPH McCARTHY

Music by
HARRY CARROLL

I'M FOREVER
BLOWING BUBBLES

SONG

BY

JAAN
KENBROVIN
AND
JOHN
WILLIAM
KELLETTE

POSED ESPECIALLY BY MISS JUNE CAPRICE, FAMOUS WM. FOX SCREEN STAR

6

New York   JEROME H. REMICK & CO.   Detroit

I'm Forever
BLOWING BUBBLES

SONG

By JAAN KENBROVIN
and
JOHN WILLIAM KELLETTE

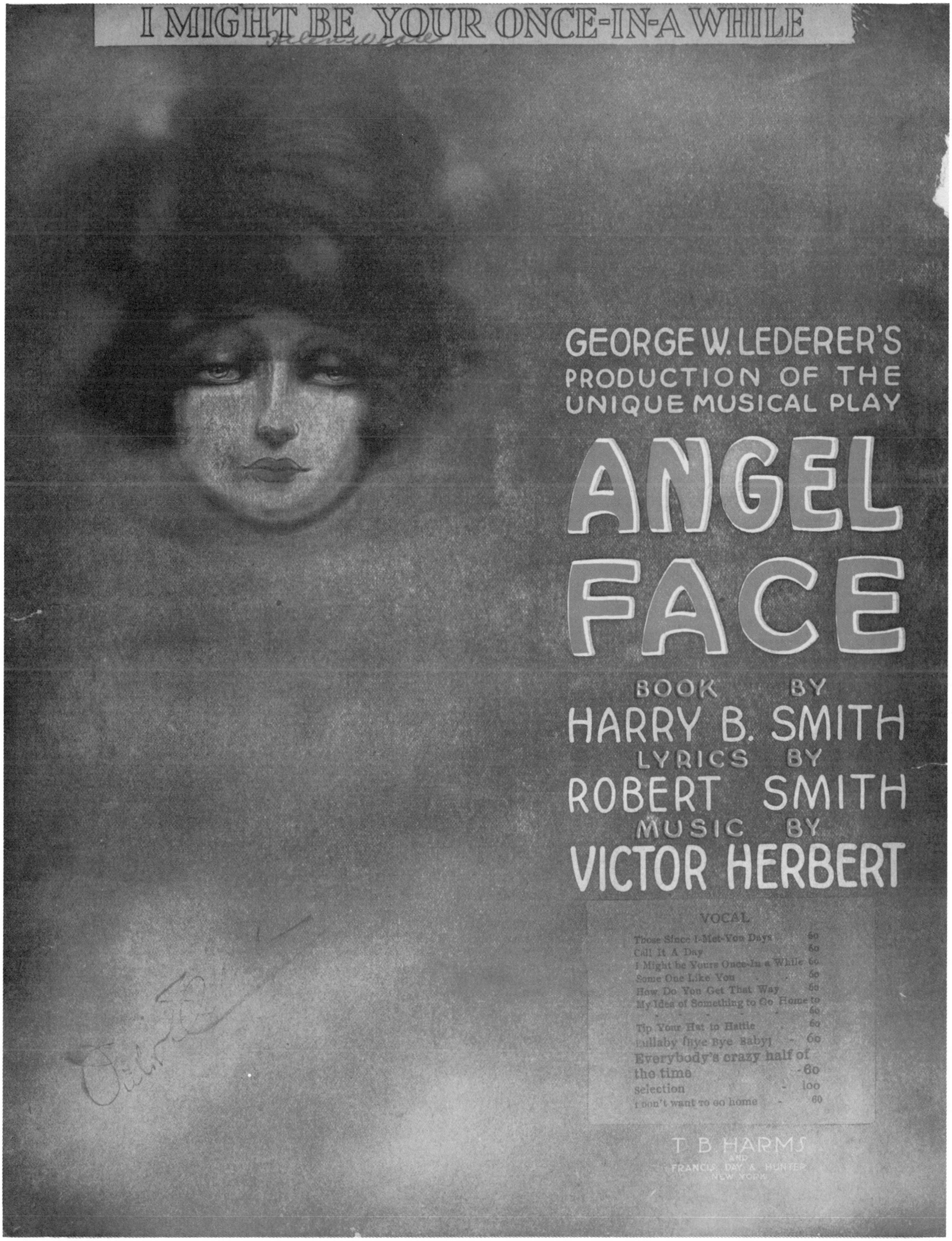

I MIGHT BE YOUR ONCE-IN-A WHILE
GEORGE W. LEDERER'S
PRODUCTION OF THE
UNIQUE MUSICAL PLAY
ANGEL
FACE
BOOK BY
HARRY B. SMITH
LYRICS BY
ROBERT SMITH
MUSIC BY
VICTOR HERBERT
VOCAL
Those Since I-Met-You Days 60
Call It A Day 60
I Might be Yours Once-In a While 60
Some One Like You 60
How Do You Get That Way 60
My Idea of Something to Go Home to 60
Tip Your Hat to Hattie 60
Lullaby (Bye Bye Baby) - 60
Everybody's crazy half of the time - 60
selection - 100
I don't want to go home - 60
T B HARMS
AND
FRANCIS DAY & HUNTER
NEW YORK

I Might Be Your "Once-In-A-While"

Lyric by
ROBERT B. SMITH

Music by
VICTOR HERBERT

stray. _____ But frank-ness is due to one Who
one. _____ I fear it's lo - cal - i - ty May

craves my ev - 'ry kiss; _____ So I make it plain in
change from day to day. _____ It is ev - 'ry where, now

my re - frain, That the best I can do is this: _____ I
here, now there, That is why I'm o - bliged to say: _____

rit. Refrain

rit. p

Poco meno
a tempo

might be your "once - in - a - while" _____ I might see you

molto espress
a tempo

once - in - a - while; _ But   I   can't   be   true   to   you   or

you   or   you.   I   can't   be   your   "all - of - the-time"   your

"ev - er   and   ev - er;"   But   may-be   your   "once-in - a-while"   will

1 do. _____   **2** I   do. _____

rit.

INDIAN SUMMER

By VICTOR HERBERT

Piano Solos

WHEN PERFORMING THIS COMPOSITION KINDLY GIVE ALL PROGRAM CREDITS TO

HARMS INC. NEW YORK, N.Y.

Indian Summer
(An American Idyl)

VICTOR HERBERT

I'VE GOT MY CAPTAIN WORKING FOR ME NOW

BY IRVING BERLIN

Irving Berlin, Inc.,
Music Publishers
1587 Broadway
New York.

I've Got My Captain Working For Me Now

By IRVING BERLIN

Marcia

Johnny Jones — was a first class private In the army last year —
He's not worth — what I have to pay him But I'll never complain —

Now he's back to bus'ness in his father's place, Sunday night I saw him with a smiling face,
I've agreed to give him fifty dollars per, It's worth twice as much to hear him call me "Sir."

When I asked — why he felt so happy, Johnny chuckled with glee; —
While I sit — in my cosy office, He's outside working hard; —

He winked his eye — and made this reply: "Something wonderful has happened to me." —
Out in the hall — at my beck and call — With a feather duster standing on guard. —

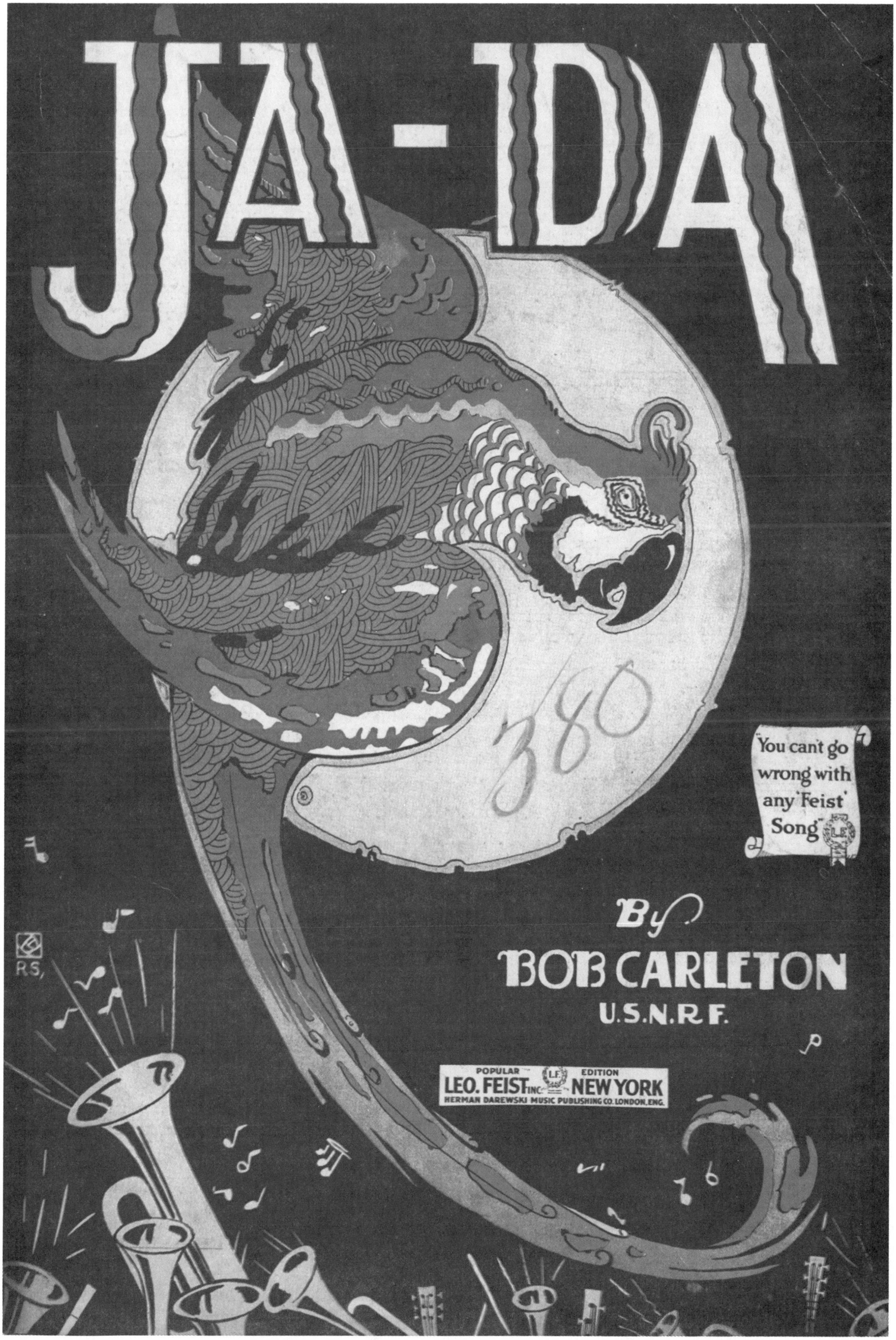
JA-DA
"You can't go wrong with any 'Feist' Song"
By
BOB CARLETON
U.S.N.R.F.
POPULAR EDITION
LEO. FEIST INC. NEW YORK
HERMAN DAREWSKI MUSIC PUBLISHING CO. LONDON, ENG.
R.S.

Ja–Da
(Ja Da, Ja Da, Jing Jing Jing!)

Words and Music by
BOB CARLETON

you've heard of your "Will O'The Wisp," But give a lit-tle lis-ten to this:___ It goes
here's a lit-tle mel-o-dy that you will find, Will lin-ger,lin-ger there in your mind:___ It goes

CHORUS With lots of Ja Da

Ja Da,___ Ja Da,___ Ja Da Ja Da Jing,Jing, Jing,___ Ja Da,___

(Ja Da,) (Ja Da,) Ev'ry-body's singing (Ja Da,)

Ja Da,___ Ja Da, Ja Da,Jing,Jing, Jing.___ That's a fun-ny lit-tle bit of

(Ja Da,)

mel - o - dy___ It's so sooth-ing and ap-peal-ing to me, It goes Ja Da,___

(Ja Da,)

Ja Da,___ Ja Da, Ja Da,Jing, Jing, Jing! Jing!

(Ja Da,)

THE SENSATIONAL STAMMERING SONG SUCCESS
SUNG BY THE SOLDIERS AND SAILORS

K-K-K-Katy

By
Geoffrey O'Hara
Army Song Leader

POPULAR EDITION
LEO. FEIST Inc. NEW YORK
HERMAN DAREWSKI MUSIC PUBLISHING CO LONDON ENG.

K-K-K- Katy

GEOFFREY O'HARA
Army Song Leader
*Composer of "Over Yonder
Where The Lilies Grow," etc.*

Jim-my was a sol - dier brave and bold,
No one ev - er looked so nice and neat,

Ka - ty was a maid with hair of gold, Like an act of fate, Kate was
No one could be just as cute and sweet, That's what Jim-my thought, When the

stand - ing at the gate, Watch - ing all the boys on dress pa - rade.
wed - ding ring he bought, Now he's off to France the foe to meet.

Jim - my with the girls was just a gawk, Stut - tered ev - 'ry
Jim - my thought he'd like to take a chance, See if he could

time he tried to talk, Still that night at eight, He was
make the Kai - ser dance, Step - ping to a tune, All a -

there at Ka - ty's gate, Stut - ter - ing to her this love sick cry.
bout the sil - v'ry moon, This is what they hear in far off France.

CHORUS

"K - K - K - Ka - ty, beau - ti - ful Ka - ty, You're the on - ly g - g - g - girl that I a -

dore; When the m - m - m - moon shines, O - ver the cow - shed, I'll be

wait - ing at the k - k - k - kitch - en door."___ "K - K - K - door."___

To Julie and Carrie

Let The Rest Of The World Go By

Words by
J. KEIRN BRENNAN

Music by
ERNEST R. BALL

Moderately with expression

With much expression

Is the strug-gle and strife We find in this life Real-ly
Is the fu-ture to hold Just strug-gles for gold While the

worth while, aft - er all?_____ I've been wish-ing to - day I could
real world waits out - side,_____ A - way out on the breast Of the

just run a - way, Out where the west winds call.____
won - der - ful West, A - cross the great Di - vide?____

REFRAIN *Tenderly with expression*

With some one like you, a pal good and true, I'd like to leave it

all be - hind, and go and find Some place that's known to God a -

lone, Just a spot to call our own. We'll find per-fect peace, Where joys nev-er cease, Out there be-neath a kind-ly sky, ___ We'll build a sweet lit-tle nest some-where in the west, And let the rest of the world go by. With by. ___

NO. 1 IN C.   NO. 2 IN D.   NO. 3 IN E♭   NO. 4 IN F.

LOVE SENDS A LITTLE GIFT OF ROSES

A BALLAD

WORDS BY

LESLIE COOKE

MUSIC BY

JOHN OPENSHAW

The following are the published arrangements of the Song and Melody.

DUET (High and Low Voices, in F) .... 60c.   TRIO (Soprano, 1st and 2nd Contralto) ..... 60c.

DUET (Mezzo and Low Voices, in E♭) ..... 60c.   MALE QUARTETTE (Octavo) .... 10c.

TRIO (Tenor, Baritone and Bass) .... 60c.   MIXED QUARTETTE (Octavo) .... 10c.

CORNET SOLO with ORCHESTRAL ACCOMPT. in E♭ .... 25c.

ORCHESTRAL ACCOMPT. for VOICE in E♭, F and C ....each 25c.

VIOLIN or CELLO OBLIGATO ALL KEYS .... each 15c.

HARMS, Incorporated
62 WEST 45th STREET, NEW YORK
CHAPPELL & CO., Ltd., LONDON, ENGLAND

MADE IN U.S.A.

Love Sends A Little Gift Of Roses

Words by
LESLIE COOKE

Music by
JOHN OPENSHAW

Take thou my gift, my of - fer - ing of ros - es,
Take thou my gift, and be it joy or sor - row,

Cull'd from my gar - den, sweet with twi - light dew;
Think ere my ros - es fade and fall a - part;

If just one flow'r up - on your breast re - pos - es
With just each sweet bloom that you may scorn to - mor - row,

Life shall for ev - er hold no rose but you.
I send to you for joy or pain my heart.

Refrain

Love sends a lit - tle gift of ros - es,

Breath - ing a pray'r un - to my pos - ies,

Torn from my heart as twi - light clos - es,

Love Sends a Little Gift of Roses

MĀDELON

(I'll Be True To The Whole Regiment)

Lyric by Louis Bousquet
English version by Alfred Bryan

SONG

Music by
Camille Robert

CHORUS

MANDY

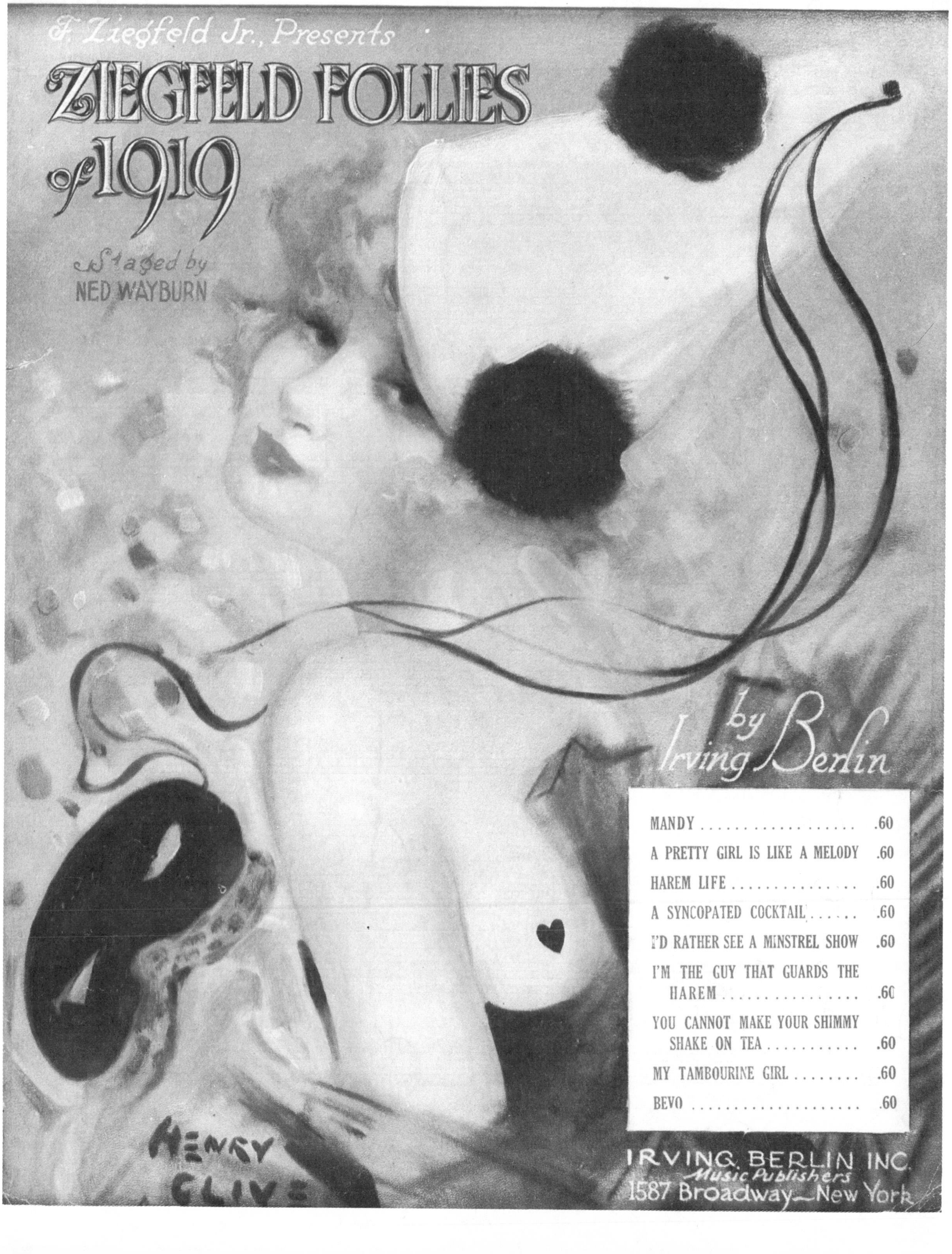
F. Ziegfeld Jr., Presents
ZIEGFELD FOLLIES of 1919
Staged by
NED WAYBURN
by Irving Berlin
MANDY .60
A PRETTY GIRL IS LIKE A MELODY .60
HAREM LIFE .60
A SYNCOPATED COCKTAIL .60
I'D RATHER SEE A MINSTREL SHOW .60
I'M THE GUY THAT GUARDS THE HAREM .60
YOU CANNOT MAKE YOUR SHIMMY SHAKE ON TEA .60
MY TAMBOURINE GIRL .60
BEVO .60
HENRY CLIVE
IRVING BERLIN INC.
Music Publishers
1587 Broadway—New York

MANDY

Words and Music by
IRVING BERLIN

I was stroll-ing out one eve - ning by the sil - v'ry moon_____ I could

MY BABY'S ARMS
F. ZIEGFELD
PRODUCTION
ZIEGFELD
FOLLIES
1919
Music By
HARRY TIERNEY
Words By
JOSEPH McCARTHY
Staged By
NED WAYBURN
6
OPERATIC EDITION
LEO. FEIST INC. NEW YORK
HERMAN DAREWSKI MUSIC PUBLISHING CO. LONDON, ENG.

My Baby's Arms

Words by
JOS. McCARTHY

Music by
HARRY TIERNEY

Moderato

I call my
It seems my

sweet-heart "Ba — by," She calls me "Ba - by," too,___
own sweet ba — by, Just loves to ba - by me.___

When there's a-ny-one near us, We nev-er let them hear us,
Tho' we both are grown up, We re-fuse to own up,

But for em - bra - ces, I know just where my place is:
She's like a moth - er, How we do love each oth - er:

CHORUS

My ba - by's arms,

Hold all my charms, My ba - by's eyes

of blue, Just seem to thrill me, And

fill me with a new sen-sa-tion, My ba-by's smile,_____

There all the while;_____ And if she'd

tell me to stay, I'd like to snug-gle a-way, And dream for-ev - er

1.

In my ba-by's arms._____

2.

arms._____

f

NOBODY KNOWS

(AND NOBODY SEEMS TO CARE)

by

IRVING BERLIN

Irving Berlin, Inc.,
Music Publishers,
1587 Broadway,
New York.

NOBODY KNOWS
(And Nobody Seems To Care)

By IRVING BERLIN

"O"
(Oh!)

Words by
BYRON GAY

BYRON GAY is the writer of "The Vamp" and "Sand Dunes"

Music by
BYRON GAY and
ARNOLD JOHNSON

I'm in the air, in the air, mean-ing at-mos-phere,
I'm glad I found, glad I found what I like the most,

Gee! she's a bear, she's a bear, let me tell you here, I'll say she's there with a
I'll stick a-round, stick a - round, like an eve-ning post, I'll nev-er stop till I

pair of most won-der-ful lips that ca-ress,____ eyes that mean "yes,"____
cop and I mar-ry my won-der-ful pet,____ I'll get her yet,____

I want to cry, want to cry, when she pass-es by, I want to die, want to
There'll be · a moon, be a moon, I mean hon-ey-moon, And we will spoon, we will

die, when I hear her sigh, Gee, Gosh - durn it I'm loon-ey I guess._____
spoon to a vamp-y tune, We'll vamp, vamp till the wed-ding is set._____

CHORUS

Oh, la-dy "O,"_____ how she can snug-gle, she's as sweet as can be,_____

And when I hold her "han-nie" "O,"_____ the way she whis-pers pret-ty

And puts me in a flur-ry, "O" _____ the way I fall for all her

beau - ti - ful lies, _____ Be-lieve me I should wor - ry, "O" _____

__ the way she feeds me taf-fy "O" _____ I think she'll drive me daf-fy, O, O, O, O,

how my sup-er-sen-ti-men-tal won-der-ful sweet-ie can love. love. __

OH BY GEE, BY GOSH, BY GUM, BY JUV

OH BY JINGO!

OH BY GEE, YOU'RE THE ONLY GIRL FOR ME

Featured by
CHARLOTTE GREENWOOD
in
OLIVER MOROSCO'S
MUSICAL PRODUCTION
Linger Longer Letty

Lyric by
LEW BROWN
Music by
ALBERT VON TILZER

PRICE SIXTY CENTS

BROADWAY MUSIC CORPORATION
WILL VON-TILZER PRESIDENT
145 WEST 45TH ST. NEW YORK

Oh! by Gee! by Gosh, by Gum, by Juv

Oh By Jingo! Oh By Gee!

You're The Only Girl For Me

Words by
LEW BROWN

Music by
ALBERT VON TILZER

You will be— our fav-'rite nut   We'll have a lot of lit-tle   Oh by Gol-lies, Then we'll put them

in the— Fol-lies   By Jin-go said, By Gosh, By Gee _____

By Jim-in-y please don't both-er me _____   So they all went a-way sing-ing

Oh by Gee, by Gosh, by Gum, by Juv by Jin-go,   by Gee you're the

on-ly girl for me.   **1.**   **2.**   me. _____   *8va*

Oh! How I Hate To Get Up In The Morning.

By IRVING BERLIN.

Oh! What A Pal Was Mary

WORDS BY
Edgar Leslie and
Bert Kalmar
MUSIC BY
Pete Wendling

PRICE 60 CENTS

BARBELLE

Waterson Berlin & Snyder Co.
STRAND THEATRE BUILDING — NEW YORK

Oh! What A Pal Was Mary

Words by
EDGAR LESLIE
& BERT KALMAR

Music by
PETE WENDLING
arr. by Fred E. Ahlert

A PRETTY GIRL IS LIKE A MELODY

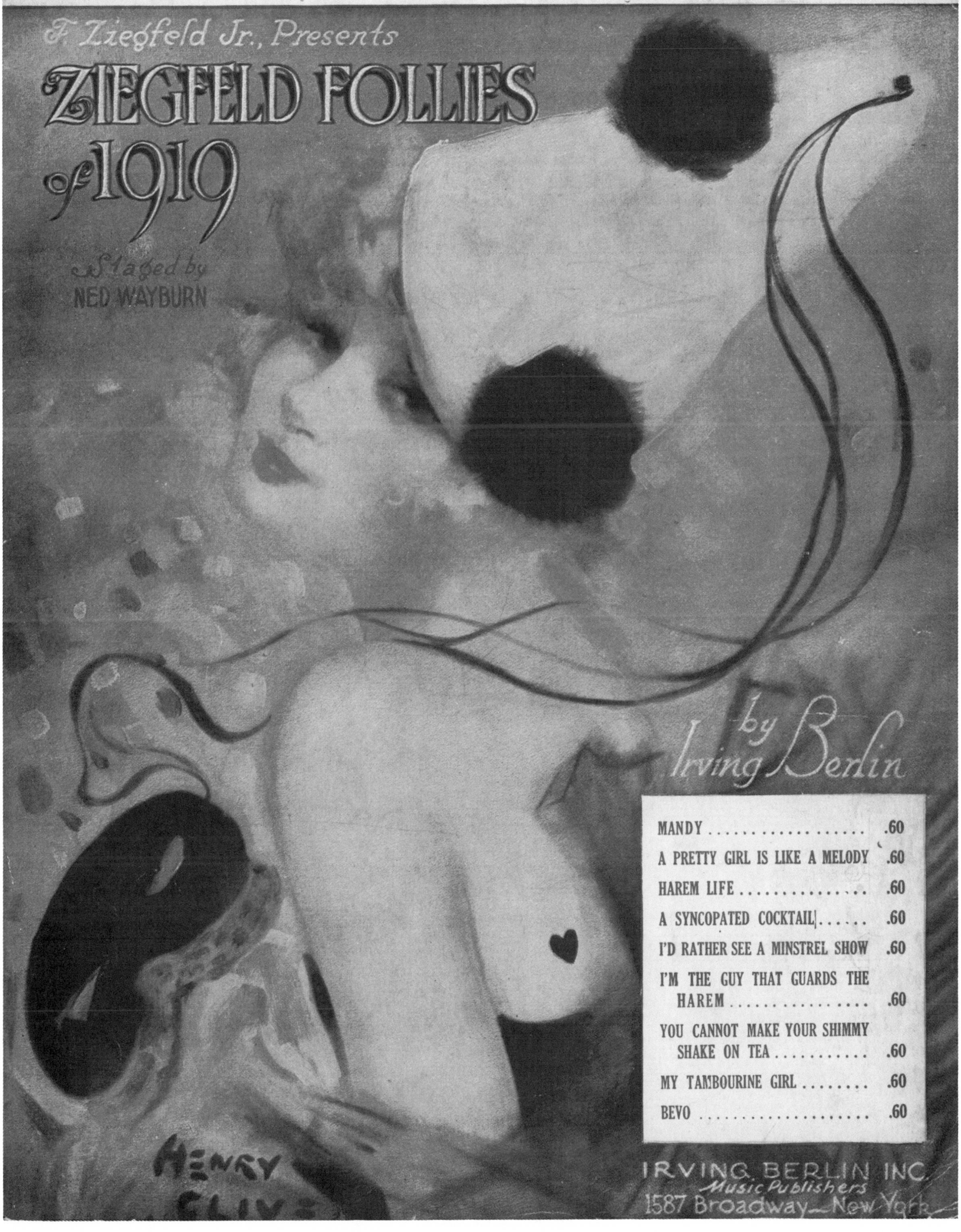

A Pretty Girl Is Like A Melody

Words and Music by
IRVING BERLIN

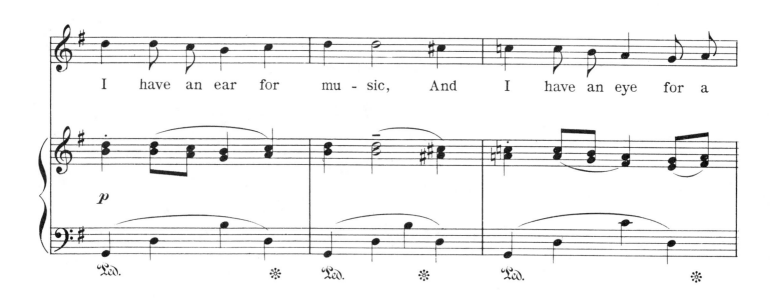

I have an ear for mu-sic, And I have an eye for a

maid I link a pret-ty girl-ie, With

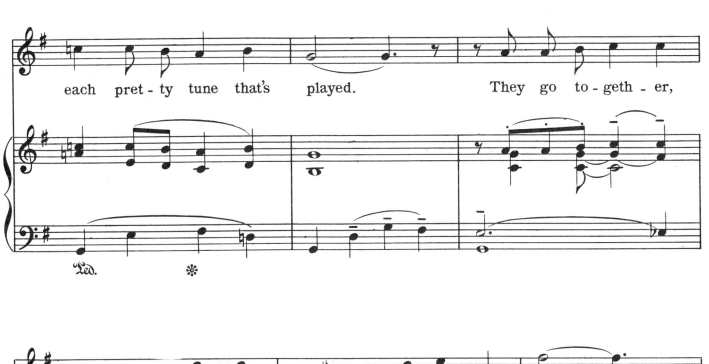

each pret - ty tune that's played. They go to - geth - er,

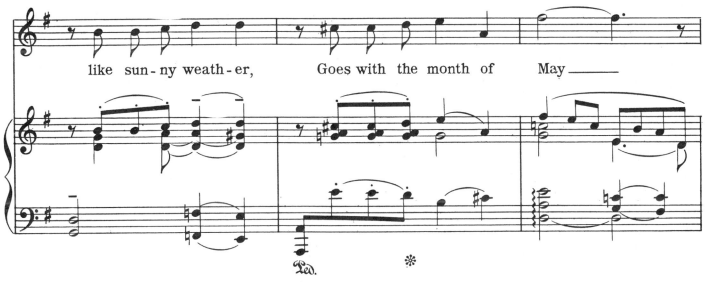

like sun - ny weath - er, Goes with the month of May

I've stu - died girls and mu - sic, So I'm qual - i - fied to say:

REFRAIN

A pret-ty girl _____ is like a mel-o-dy _____ That haunts you night and day _____ Just like the strain of a haunt-ing re-frain, She'll start up-on a mar-a-thon And run a-round your brain, You can't es - cape _____

108 *A Pretty Girl Is Like a Melody*

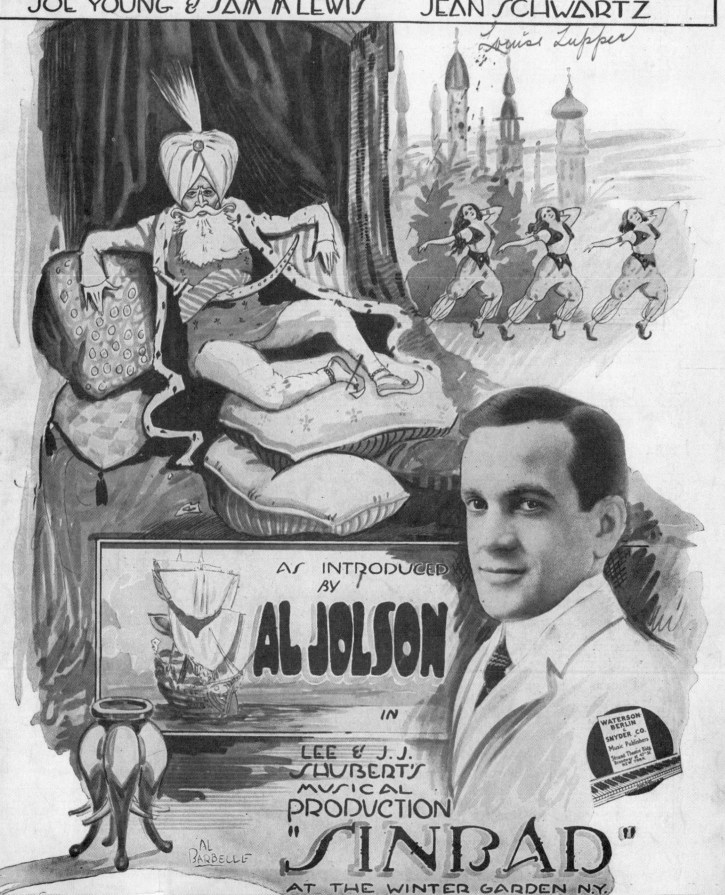

Rock-a-Bye Your Baby With A Dixie Melody

Words by
SAM M. LEWIS
and JOE YOUNG

Music by
JEAN SCHWARTZ

THE·ROSE·OF
NOMANS·LAND
Words by
Jack Caddigan
POPULAR EDITION
LEO FEIST Inc. New York
Herman Darewski Music Publishing Co London, Eng.
Music by
James A. Brennan

THE ROSE OF NO MAN'S LAND

(Jack)   (Jas. A.)
By CADDIGAN and BRENNAN
Writers of "We're all going calling on the Kaiser"

I've seen some beau-ti-ful flow-ers, Grow in life's gar-den
Out of the heav-en-ly splen-dor, Down to the trail of

fair, I've spent some won-der-ful hours Lost in their fra-grance
woe, God in his mer-cy has sent her Cheer-ing the world be-

rare, But I have found an-oth-er Won-drous be-yond com-pare.
low We call her Rose of Heav-en We've learn'd to love her so.

Standard
Rose Room
Song
Words by
Harry Williams
Music by
Art Hickman
.30 NET
W. R.
DE LAPPE
Sherman, Clay & Co.
SAN FRANCISCO

ROSE ROOM
(FOX TROT)
SONG
In Sunny Roseland

Lyrics by
HARRY WILLIAMS

Music by
ART HICKMAN

Moderato

I want to take you to a
The ball is o - ver and the

lit - tle room,   A lit - tle room where all the ros - es bloom.
tu - lips meet,   Their lit - tle kiss - es are so short and sweet.

I want to lead you in - to Na - ture's Hall,   Where ev - 'ry year the ros - es
The lil - ies nod to the for - get - me - nots,   When they're de - part - ing in their

give a ball.—   They have an Or - ches - tra up in the trees,—
flow - er pots.—   But all the ros - es with their spir - its high,—

For their mu-si-cians are the birds and bees.— And they will
Re-main to love un-til they droop and die.— And dear, why

sing us a song As we are stroll-ing a-long.— In sun-ny
should-n't it be Just so with you and with me.— In sun-ny

CHORUS *Slowly*

rose - land, where sum-mer breez-es are play - - ing,

Where the hon-ey bees are "a May - - ing"

There———— all the ros-es are sway - - ing,

Danc - ing____ while the mead-ow brook flows.____ The moon when shin - ing

Is more than ev - er de - sign - - ing, For

'tis ev-er then I am pin - ing, Pin - ing____

— to be sweet-ly re-clin - ing Some-where in Rose - land,

Be - side a beau-ti-ful Rose.____ I sun - ny Rose.____

Smiles
Jerome H.
Remick & Co.
Detroit
New York
5
Words by
J. Will Callahan
Music by
Lee S. Roberts

SMILES

Lyric by
J. WILL CALLAHAN

Music by
LEE S. ROBERTS

Copyright, 1917, by Lee S. Roberts, Fine Arts Bldg., Chicago, Ill
Transferred 1918 to Jerome H. Remick & Co., Detroit & New York

International copyright secured

REFRAIN

smiles _____ that make us hap - py, _____ There are smiles _____ that make us blue, _____ There are smiles _____ that steal a-way the tear - drops. _____ As the sun - beams steal a-way the dew, _____ There are smiles ___ that have a ten-der mean - ing _____ That the eyes ___ of love a-lone may see, _____ And the smiles ___ that fill my life with sun - shine _____ Are the smiles that you give to me _____ There are me _____

Souvenir Edition

Smilin' Through

Introduced in
Joseph M. Schenck's
Motion Picture Version
of the
Fantastic Play
"Smilin'
Through"

featuring
*Norma
Talmadge*

A First National Attraction

SOLO — FIVE KEYS
C (c to d); D, (d to e); Eb,(eb to f); F,(f to g); G,(g to a);
DUET — TWO KEYS, C and Eb

Lyric and Music by
Arthur A. Penn

M. Witmark & Sons
New York

60¢ net   Printed in U.S.A.

UNIQUE CONTROVERSY ENDS IN COMPROMISE

SO great has been the popularity of **"SMILIN' THROUGH"** from the beginning, that the publishers found themselves besieged with requests from all over the country for a third verse, on the ground that the song "was too good to be so short." At our request, Mr. Penn, the author and composer of **"SMILIN' THROUGH,"** wrote an added stanza, which resulted in one of the most interesting and country-wide controversies that ever originated over a song. Both the publishers and the composer were inundated with appeals on the one hand to add the new verse permanently to **"SMILIN' THROUGH";** while on the other, thousands of admirers urged them to leave the song as it was. The controversy continued for months, with the significant result that when the final opinions from singers, teachers, and the public generally were counted, they were found to be practically evenly divided. After carefully weighing the arguments pro and con, the following happy compromise has been decided on :—

To leave **"SMILIN' THROUGH"** in its original form and with its original ending, as a complete song; but, for the satisfaction and convenience of those who desire to use the Extra Verse, the words are here printed. This verse is sung to the music and accompaniment of the Second Verse.

THE PUBLISHERS.

THE EXTRA STANZA

III

And if ever I'm left in this world all alone,
I shall wait for my call patiently;
For if Heaven be kind,
I shall wake there to find
Those two eyes o' blue
Still smilin' through
At me!

Smilin' Through

There's a little brown road windin' over the hill
To a little white cot by the sea;
There's a little green gate
At whose trellis I wait,
While two eyes o' blue
Come smilin' through
At me!

There's a gray lock or two in the brown of the hair,
There's some silver in mine, too, I see;
But in all the long years
When the clouds brought their tears,
Those two eyes o' blue
Kept smilin' through
At me!

Arthur A. Penn

Smilin' Through

Lyric and Music
By ARTHUR A. PENN

There's a lit-tle brown road wind-in' o - ver the hill To a lit-tle white cot by the sea; There's a

lit - tle green gate At whose trel - lis I wait, While two

eyes o' blue Come smil-in' through At me!_____ There's a

gray lock or two in the brown of the hair, There's some

sil - ver in mine, too, I see; _____ But in

all the long years When the clouds brought their tears, Those two

eyes o' blue Kept smil - in' through At me! _____

SOMEBODY STOLE MY GAL.
By LEO WOOD
Chorus
Somebody stole my Gal,
Somebody stole my Pal.
Somebody came and took her away,
She didn't even say she was leavin
The kisses I Loved so
He's getting now I know,
And Gee, I know that she
Would come to me
If she could see
Her broken hearted lonesome pal,
Somebody stole my Gal.
SUNG BY
FLORENCE
MILETT
The Phenomenal Soprano
Vocalist with the
LADY BOUNTIFUL MINSTRELS
MEYER COHEN MUSIC PUB. CO. INC
1531 BROADWAY, NEW YORK

Somebody Stole My Gal

By LEO WOOD

Gee, but I'm lone-some, lone-some and blue__ I've found out some-thing I nev-er knew__
An-gels they say are on-ly a-bove__ I know that's wrong be-cause my old love__

I know now what it means to be sad__ For I've lost the best__ gal I ev-er had;__
Sure is an an-gel take it from me__ And she's all the an-gel I want to see;__

She on-ly left__ yes-ter-day_____ Some-bo-dy stole her a-way.__
May be she'll come__ back some day_____ All I can do__ now is pray.__

SWANEE

WORDS BY **I. CAESAR** MUSIC BY **GEORGE GERSHWIN**

Successfully Introduced
by
AL JOLSON
in
"SINBAD"
at the
Winter Garden
New York

6

T. B. HARMS
AND
FRANCIS, DAY & HUNTER
NEW YORK

Swanee

Words by
I. CAESAR

Music by
GEORGE GERSHWIN

I've been a - way from you a long time ___ I nev - er

thought I'd miss you so ___ Some - how I feel

Your love was real Near you I long to be ___

The birds are sing-ing It is song-time ___ The ban-jos

strum-min' soft and low ___ I know that you Yearn for me

too Swan - ee You're call - ing me.

Refrain

Swan - ee How I love you How I love you My

dear old Swan-ee _____ I'd give the world to be

A - mong the folks in D - I - X - I - E - ven know my

Mam - my's Wait-ing for me Pray-ing for me Down by the

Swan-ee _____ The folks up north will see me no more _____ When

Till We Meet Again
Song
LYRIC BY
RAYMOND B. EGAN
MUSIC BY
RICHARD A. WHITING
FSM
5
Jerome H. Remick & Co.,
DETROIT ~ NEW YORK

TILL WE MEET AGAIN

Lyric by
RAYMOND B. EGAN

Song

Music by
RICHARD A. WHITING

Slowly

PIANO

VOICE

There's a song in the land of the li - ly _____ Each sweet-heart has
Tho' good-bye means the birth of a tear drop _____ Hel - lo means the

heard with a sigh _____ O - ver high gar - den walls This
birth of a smile _____ And the smile will e - rase The

sweet e - cho falls As a sol-dier boy whispers good-bye _____
tear blight-ing trace When we meet in the af - ter - a - while _____

poco ritard.

   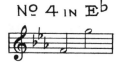

NO 5 DUET

SOPRANO OR TENOR
ALTO OR BARITONE

THE WORLD IS WAITING FOR THE SUNRISE

SONG

WORDS BY

EUGENE LOCKHART

MUSIC BY

ERNEST SEITZ

PRICE 50 CENTS NET
EXCEPTING CANADA AND FOREIGN COUNTRIES

ALSO PUBLISHED FOR

TWO PART FEMALE VOICES	(S.S.) .15	FOUR PART MIXED VOICES (S.A.T.B.)	.15
THREE PART FEMALE VOICES	(S.S.A.) .15	FOUR PART MALE VOICES (T.T.B.B.)	.15

CHAPPELL & Co., Inc.

RKO BUILDING – ROCKEFELLER CENTER

NEW YORK, N.Y.

CHAPPELL & Co., Ltd.

LONDON ——— PARIS

SYDNEY

PRINTED IN U.S.A.

VOLKWEIN'S
632 LIBERTY AVENUE
PITTSBURGH, PA.

The World Is Waiting For The Sunrise

Ukulele arr. by May Singhi Breen

SONG

Words by
EUGENE LOCKHART

May be had on all
Records, Piano & Word-Rolls

Music by
ERNEST SEITZ

Tune Ukulele

G C E A

Rather Slowly

Down in the la-zy west rides the moon, Warm as a night in June; Stars shimm-'ring soft in a bed of blue, While I am call-ing and call-ing you. Sweet-ly you are

Symbols for Guitar
arr. by S.M. Zoltai

YOU'D BE SURPRISED

AS FEATURED BY
IRVING BERLIN
EDDIE CANTOR
in "Ziegfeld Follies"
GEORGE JESSEL
in "Shubert Gaieties at Winter Garden"
LEW COOPER
in "Oh! What A Girl"

By
Irving Berlin

PRICE 60 CENTS

Irving Berlin, Inc.
Music Publishers
1587 Broadway
New York.

You'd Be Surprised

By IRVING BERLIN

How she could pick such a beau. With a twink-le in her eye.___ She made this re - ply.___
He has the bus - i - est phone Al-most ev - 'ry oth-er day.___ A new girl will say.___

CHORUS

He's not so good in a crowd but when you get him a - lone   You'd be sur -
He's not so good in the house but on a bench in the park   You'd be sur -

prised,___ He is - n't much at a dance But then when he takes you home
prised,___ He is - n't much in the light but when he gets in the dark

You'd be sur - prised___ He does-n't look like much of a lov - er, but
You'd be sur - prised___ I know he looks as slow as the E - rie But

don't judge a book by it's cov - er.   He's got the face of an An - gel but
you do'nt know the half of it dearie   He looks as cold as an Es - ki - mo

There's a Dev-il in his eye. He's such a del-i-cate thing but when he
But there's fi-re in his eyes He does-n't say ver-y much but when he

starts in to squeeze, You'd be sur - prised, He does-n't
starts in to speak You'd be sur - prised, He's not so

look ver-y strong but when you sit on his knee, You'd be sur - prised
good at the start but at the end of a week You'd be sur - prised

At a par-ty or at a ball I've got to ad-mit he's noth-ing at all but in a
On a street-car or in a train You'd think he was born with-out an-y brain, but in a

mor ris chair, You'd be sur - prised. He's not so prised.
tax-i - cab, You'd be sur - prised He's not so prised

OPERATIC-EDITION

HIGH KEY A♭

SOPRANO OR TENOR

MEDIUM KEY F

MEZZO OR BARITONE

LOW KEY E♭

ALTO OR BASS

YOUR EYES HAVE TOLD ME SO

SONG

LYRIC BY

GUSTAVE KAHN

AND

EGBERT VAN ALSTYNE

MUSIC BY

WALTER BLAUFUSS

PRICE 60 CENTS

JEROME H. REMICK & CO.

DETROIT   NEW YORK

YOUR EYES HAVE TOLD ME SO

SONG

Lyric by
GUS KAHN and
EGBERT VAN ALSTYNE

Music by
WALTER BLAUFUSS

Your Eyes Have Told Me So

OPERATIC EDITION
You Said It
WORDS BY
BERT KALMAR
& EDDIE COX
MUSIC BY
HENRY SANTLEY
Waterson, Berlin & Snyder Co.
STRAND THEATRE BUILDING
NEW YORK
Barbelle

YOU SAID IT!

Words by
BERT KALMAR
and EDDIE COX

Music by
HENRY W. SANTLEY

out;—— And when they lay their eyes on her,—— You will hear them shout:——
day;—— You'll hear the school-boys sing-ing this,—— While they are at play:——

Chorus

"Is she sort of cute and pret-ty? You said it! Would she shine in

a-ny ci-ty? You said it! Has she got beau-ti-ful clothes?——

Has she got plen-ty of beaux?— And has she lots of oth-er things that

no - bod - y   knows? You said it!   Would she make you spend your mon-ey? You said it!

Would she fill your   lit - tle heart with   joy? _____

She's the ver - y   kind you bet, ___   Ev - 'ry fel - low   wants to pet, ___
When you call her   on   the 'phone, ___   And she tells you   she's a - lone, ___
All the wild men she just tames, ___   Makes them call her   pret - ty names, ___

Is she ve - ry   hard to get? ___
Would you leave your hap - py home? ___ You said it,   boy!" ___   boy!" ___
Could she cap - ture Jes - sie James? ___

D.S.

Dover Piano and Keyboard Editions

THE WELL-TEMPERED CLAVIER: Books I and II, Complete, Johann Sebastian Bach. All 48 preludes and fugues in all major and minor keys. Authoritative Bach-Gesellschaft edition. Explanation of ornaments in English, tempo indications, music corrections. 208pp. 9⅜ × 12¼. 24532-2 Pa. **$9.95**

KEYBOARD MUSIC, J. S. Bach. Bach-Gesellschaft edition. For harpsichord, piano, other keyboard instruments. English Suites, French Suites, Six Partitas, Goldberg Variations, Two-Part Inventions, Three-Part Sinfonias. 312pp. 8⅛ × 11. 22360-4 Pa. **$11.95**

ITALIAN CONCERTO, CHROMATIC FANTASIA AND FUGUE AND OTHER WORKS FOR KEYBOARD, Johann Sebastian Bach. Sixteen of Bach's best-known, most-performed and most-recorded works for the keyboard, reproduced from the authoritative Bach-Gesellschaft edition. 112pp. 9 × 12. 25387-2 Pa. **$8.95**

COMPLETE KEYBOARD TRANSCRIPTIONS OF CONCERTOS BY BAROQUE COMPOSERS, Johann Sebastian Bach. Sixteen concertos by Vivaldi, Telemann and others, transcribed for solo keyboard instruments. Bach-Gesellschaft edition. 128pp. 9⅜ × 12¼. 25529-8 Pa. **$8.95**

ORGAN MUSIC, J. S. Bach. Bach-Gesellschaft edition. 93 works. 6 Trio Sonatas, German Organ Mass, Orgelbüchlein, Six Schubler Chorales, 18 Choral Preludes. 357pp. 8⅛ × 11. 22359-0 Pa. **$12.95**

COMPLETE PRELUDES AND FUGUES FOR ORGAN, Johann Sebastian Bach. All 25 of Bach's complete sets of preludes and fugues (i.e. compositions written as pairs), from the authoritative Bach-Gesellschaft edition. 168pp. 8⅜ × 11. 24816-X Pa. **$9.95**

TOCCATAS, FANTASIAS, PASSACAGLIA AND OTHER WORKS FOR ORGAN, J. S. Bach. Over 20 best-loved works including Toccata and Fugue in D minor, BWV 565; Passacaglia and Fugue in C minor, BWV 582, many more. Bach-Gesellschaft edition. 176pp. 9 × 12. 25403-8 Pa. **$9.95**

TWO- AND THREE-PART INVENTIONS, J. S. Bach. Reproduction of original autograph ms. Edited by Eric Simon. 62pp. 8⅛ × 11. 21982-8 Pa. **$8.95**

THE 36 FANTASIAS FOR KEYBOARD, Georg Philipp Telemann. Graceful compositions by 18th-century master. 1923 Breslauer edition. 80pp. 8⅛ × 11. 25365-1 Pa. **$5.95**

GREAT KEYBOARD SONATAS, Carl Philipp Emanuel Bach. Comprehensive two-volume edition contains 51 sonatas by second, most important son of Johann Sebastian Bach. Originality, rich harmony, delicate workmanship. Authoritative French edition. Total of 384pp. 8⅜ × 11¼. Series I 24853-4 Pa. **$9.95**
Series II 24854-2 Pa. **$10.95**

KEYBOARD WORKS/Series One: Ordres I–XIII; Series Two: Ordres XIV–XXVII and Miscellaneous Pieces, François Couperin. Over 200 pieces. Reproduced directly from edition prepared by Johannes Brahms and Friedrich Chrysander. Total of 496pp. 8⅜ × 11.
Series I 25795-9 Pa. **$10.95**
Series II 25796-7 Pa. **$11.95**

KEYBOARD WORKS FOR SOLO INSTRUMENTS, G. F. Handel. 35 neglected works from Handel's vast oeuvre, originally jotted down as improvisations. Includes Eight Great Suites, others. New sequence. 174pp. 9⅜ × 12¼. 24338-9 Pa. **$9.95**

WORKS FOR ORGAN AND KEYBOARD, Jan Pieterszoon Sweelinck. Nearly all of early Dutch composer's difficult-to-find keyboard works. Chorale variations; toccatas, fantasias; variations on secular, dance tunes. Also, incomplete and/or modified works, plus fantasia by John Bull. 272pp. 9 × 12. 24935-2 Pa. **$12.95**

ORGAN WORKS, Dietrich Buxtehude. Complete organ works of extremely influential pre-Bach composer. Toccatas, preludes, chorales, more. Definitive Breitkopf & Härtel edition. 320pp. 8⅜ × 11¼. (Available in U.S. only) 25682-0 Pa. **$12.95**

THE FUGUES ON THE MAGNIFICAT FOR ORGAN OR KEYBOARD, Johann Pachelbel. 94 pieces representative of Pachelbel's magnificent contribution to keyboard composition; can be played on the organ, harpsichord or piano. 100pp. 9 × 12. (Available in U.S. only) 25037-7 Pa. **$7.95**

MY LADY NEVELLS BOOKE OF VIRGINAL MUSIC, William Byrd. 42 compositions in modern notation from 1591 ms. For any keyboard instrument. 245pp. 8⅛ × 11. 22246-2 Pa. **$13.95**

ELIZABETH ROGERS HIR VIRGINALL BOOKE, edited with calligraphy by Charles J. F. Cofone. All 112 pieces from noted 1656 manuscript, most never before published. Composers include Thomas Brewer, William Byrd, Orlando Gibbons, etc. 125pp. 9 × 12. 23138-0 Pa. **$10.95**

THE FITZWILLIAM VIRGINAL BOOK, edited by J. Fuller Maitland, W. B. Squire. Famous early 17th-century collection of keyboard music, 300 works by Morley, Byrd, Bull, Gibbons, etc. Modern notation. Total of 938pp. 8⅜ × 11. Two-vol. set. 21068-5, 21069-3 Pa. **$33.90**

GREAT KEYBOARD SONATAS, Series I and Series II, Domenico Scarlatti. 78 of the most popular sonatas reproduced from the G. Ricordi edition edited by Alessandro Longo. Total of 320pp. 8⅜ × 11¼.
Series I 24996-4 Pa. **$8.95**
Series II 25003-2 Pa. **$8.95**

SONATAS AND FANTASIES FOR THE PIANO, W. A. Mozart, edited by Nathan Broder. Finest, most accurate edition, based on autographs and earliest editions. 19 sonatas, plus Fantasy and Fugue in C, K.394, Fantasy in C Minor, K.396, Fantasy in D Minor, K.397. 352pp. 9 × 12. (Available in U.S. only) 25417-8 Pa. **$16.50**

COMPLETE PIANO SONATAS, Joseph Haydn. 52 sonatas reprinted from authoritative Breitkopf & Härtel edition. Extremely clear and readable; ample space for notes, analysis. 464pp. 9⅜ × 12¼.
24726-0 Pa. **$10.95**
24727-9 Pa. **$11.95**

BAGATELLES, RONDOS AND OTHER SHORTER WORKS FOR PIANO, Ludwig van Beethoven. Most popular and most performed shorter works, including Rondo a capriccio in G and Andante in F. Breitkopf & Härtel edition. 128pp. 9⅜ × 12¼. 25392-9 Pa. **$8.95**

COMPLETE VARIATIONS FOR SOLO PIANO, Ludwig van Beethoven. Contains all 21 sets of Beethoven's piano variations, including the extremely popular *Diabelli Variations, Op. 120*. 240pp. 9⅜ × 12¼. 25188-8 Pa. **$11.95**

COMPLETE PIANO SONATAS, Ludwig van Beethoven. All sonatas in fine Schenker edition, with fingering, analytical material. One of best modern editions. 615pp. 9 × 12. Two-vol. set. 23134-8, 23135-6 Pa. **$25.90**

COMPLETE SONATAS FOR PIANOFORTE SOLO, Franz Schubert. All 15 sonatas. Breitkopf and Härtel edition. 293pp. 9⅜ × 12¼. 22647-6 Pa. **$13.95**

DANCES FOR SOLO PIANO, Franz Schubert. Over 350 waltzes, minuets, landler, ecossaises, other charming, melodic dance compositions reprinted from the authoritative Breitkopf & Härtel edition. 192pp. 9⅜ × 12¼. 26107-7 Pa. **$10.95**

*Available from your music dealer or write for **free** Music Catalog to Dover Publications, Inc., Dept. MUBI, 31 East 2nd Street, Mineola, N.Y. 11501.*

ORGAN WORKS, César Franck. Composer's best-known works for organ, including Six Pieces, Trois Pieces, and Trois Chorals. Oblong format for easy use at keyboard. Authoritative Durand edition. 208pp. 11⅜ × 8¼. 25517-4 Pa. **$12.95**

IBERIA AND ESPAÑA: Two Complete Works for Solo Piano, Isaac Albeniz. Spanish composer's greatest piano works in authoritative editions. Includes the popular "Tango". 192pp. 9 × 12. 25367-8 Pa. **$10.95**

GOYESCAS, SPANISH DANCES AND OTHER WORKS FOR SOLO PIANO, Enrique Granados. Great Spanish composer's most admired, most performed suites for the piano, in definitive Spanish editions. 176pp. 9 × 12. 25481-X Pa. **$8.95**

SELECTED PIANO COMPOSITIONS, César Franck, edited by Vincent d'Indy. Outstanding selection of influential French composer's piano works, including early pieces and the two masterpieces—Prelude, Choral and Fugue; and Prelude, Aria and Finale. Ten works in all. 138pp. 9 × 12. 23269-7 Pa. **$10.95**

THE COMPLETE PRELUDES AND ETUDES FOR PIANOFORTE SOLO, Alexander Scriabin. All the preludes and études including many perfectly spun miniatures. Edited by K. N. Igumnov and Y. I. Mil'shteyn. 250pp. 9 × 12. 22919-X Pa. **$10.95**

COMPLETE PIANO SONATAS, Alexander Scriabin. All ten of Scriabin's sonatas, reprinted from an authoritative early Russian edition. 256pp. 8⅜ × 11¼. 25850-5 Pa. **$11.95**

COMPLETE PRELUDES AND ETUDES-TABLEAUX, Serge Rachmaninoff. Forty-one of his greatest works for solo piano, including the riveting C minor, G-minor and B-minor preludes, in authoritative editions. 208pp. 8⅜ × 11¼. 25696-0 Pa. **$10.95**

COMPLETE PIANO SONATAS, Sergei Prokofiev. Definitive Russian edition of nine sonatas (1907–1953), among the most important compositions in the modern piano repertoire. 288pp. 8⅜ × 11¼. (Available in U.S. only) 25689-8 Pa. **$11.95**

GYMNOPÉDIES, GNOSSIENNES AND OTHER WORKS FOR PIANO, Erik Satie. The largest Satie collection of piano works yet published, 17 in all, reprinted from the original French editions. 176pp. 9 × 12. (Not available in France or Germany) 25978-1 Pa. **$9.95**

TWENTY SHORT PIECES FOR PIANO (Sports et Divertissements), Erik Satie. French master's brilliant thumbnail sketches—verbal and musical—of various outdoor sports and amusements. English translations, 20 illustrations. Rare, limited 1925 edition. 48pp. 12 × 8⅞. (Not available in France or Germany) 24365-6 Pa. **$5.95**

COMPLETE PRELUDES, IMPROMPTUS AND VALSES-CAPRICES, Gabriel Fauré. Eighteen elegantly wrought piano works in authoritative editions. Only one-volume collection. 144pp. 9 × 12. (Not available in France or Germany) 25789-4 Pa. **$8.95**

PIANO MUSIC OF BÉLA BARTÓK, Series I, Béla Bartók. New, definitive Archive Edition incorporating composer's corrections. Includes *Funeral March* from *Kossuth*, *Fourteen Bagatelles*, Bartók's break to modernism. 167pp. 9 × 12. (Available in U.S. only) 24108-4 Pa. **$10.95**

PIANO MUSIC OF BÉLA BARTÓK, Series II, Béla Bartók. Second in the Archie Edition incorporating composer's corrections. 85 short pieces *For Children, Two Elegies, Two Rumanian Dances*, etc. 192pp. 9 × 12. (Available in U.S. only) 24109-2 Pa. **$10.95**

FRENCH PIANO MUSIC, AN ANTHOLOGY, Isidor Phillipp (ed.). 44 complete works, 1670–1905, by Lully, Couperin, Rameau, Alkan, Saint-Saëns, Delibes, Bizet, Godard, many others; favorites, lesser-known examples, but all top quality. 188pp. 9 × 12. (Not available in France or Germany) 23381-2 Pa. **$9.95**

NINETEENTH-CENTURY EUROPEAN PIANO MUSIC: Unfamiliar Masterworks, John Gillespie (ed.). Difficult-to-find études, toccatas, polkas, impromptus, waltzes, etc., by Albéniz, Bizet, Chabrier, Fauré, Smetana, Richard Strauss, Wagner and 16 other composers. 62 pieces. 343pp. 9 × 12. (Not available in France or Germany) 23447-9 Pa. **$15.95**

RARE MASTERPIECES OF RUSSIAN PIANO MUSIC: Eleven Pieces by Glinka, Balakirev, Glazunov and Others, edited by Dmitry Feofanov. Glinka's *Prayer*, Balakirev's *Reverie*, Liapunov's *Transcendental Etude, Op. 11, No. 10*, and eight others—full, authoritative scores from Russian texts. 144pp. 9 × 12. 24659-0 Pa. **$8.95**

HUMORESQUES AND OTHER WORKS FOR SOLO PIANO, Antonín Dvořák. Humoresques, Op. 101, complete, Silhouettes, Op. 8, Poetic Tone Pictures, Theme with Variations, Op. 36, 4 Slavonic Dances, more. 160pp. 9 × 12. 28355-0 Pa. **$9.95**

PIANO MUSIC, Louis M. Gottschalk. 26 pieces (including covers) by early 19th-century American genius. "Bamboula," "The Banjo," other Creole, Negro-based material, through elegant salon music. 301pp. 9¼ × 12. 21683-7 Pa. **$13.95**

SOUSA'S GREAT MARCHES IN PIANO TRANSCRIPTION, John Philip Sousa. Playing edition includes: "The Stars and Stripes Forever," "King Cotton," "Washington Post," much more. 24 illustrations. 111pp. 9 × 12. 23132-1 Pa. **$7.95**

COMPLETE PIANO RAGS, Scott Joplin. All 38 piano rags by the acknowledged master of the form, reprinted from the publisher's original editions complete with sheet music covers. Introduction by David A. Jasen. 208pp. 9 × 12. 25807-6 Pa. **$9.95**

RAGTIME REDISCOVERIES, selected by Trebor Jay Tichenor. 64 unusual rags demonstrate diversity of style, local tradition. Original sheet music. 320pp. 9 × 12. 23776-1 Pa. **$14.95**

RAGTIME RARITIES, edited by Trebor J. Tichenor. 63 tuneful, rediscovered piano rags by 51 composers (or teams). Does not duplicate selections in *Classic Piano Rags* (Dover, 20469-3). 305pp. 9 × 12. 23157-7 Pa. **$12.95**

CLASSIC PIANO RAGS, selected with an introduction by Rudi Blesh. Best ragtime music (1897–1922) by Scott Joplin, James Scott, Joseph F. Lamb, Tom Turpin, nine others. 364pp. 9 × 12. 20469-3 Pa. **$14.95**

RAGTIME GEMS: Original Sheet Music for 25 Ragtime Classics, edited by David A. Jasen. Includes original sheet music and covers for 25 rags, including three of Scott Joplin's finest: *Searchlight Rag, Rose Leaf Rag* and *Fig Leaf Rag*. 122pp. 9 × 12. 25248-5 Pa. **$7.95**

NOCTURNES AND BARCAROLLES FOR SOLO PIANO, Gabriel Fauré. 12 nocturnes and 12 barcarolles reprinted from authoritative French editions. 208pp. 9⅜ × 12¼. (Not available in France or Germany) 27955-3 Pa. **$10.95**

PRELUDES AND FUGUES FOR PIANO, Dmitry Shostakovich. 24 Preludes, Op. 34 and 24 Preludes and Fugues, Op. 87. Reprint of Gosudarstvennoe Izdatel'stvo Muzyka, Moscow, ed. 288pp. 8⅜ × 11. (Available in U.S. only) 26861-6 Pa. **$12.95**

FAVORITE WALTZES, POLKAS AND OTHER DANCES FOR SOLO PIANO, Johann Strauss, Jr. Blue Danube, Tales from Vienna Woods, many other best-known waltzes and other dances. 160pp. 9 × 12. 27851-4 Pa. **$10.95**

SELECTED PIANO WORKS FOR FOUR HANDS, Franz Schubert. 24 separate pieces (16 most popular titles): Three Military Marches, Lebensstürme, Four Polonaises, Four Ländler, etc. Rehearsal numbers added. 273pp. 9 × 12. 23529-7 Pa. **$12.95**

Dover Piano and Keyboard Editions

SHORTER WORKS FOR PIANOFORTE SOLO, Franz Schubert. All piano music except Sonatas, Dances, and a few unfinished pieces. Contains Wanderer, Impromptus, Moments Musicals, Variations, Scherzi, etc. Breitkopf and Härtel edition. 199pp. 9⅜ × 12¼.
22648-4 Pa. **$10.95**

WALTZES AND SCHERZOS, Frédéric Chopin. All of the Scherzos and nearly all (20) of the Waltzes from the authoritative Paderewski edition. Editorial commentary. 214pp. 9 × 12. (Available in U.S. only)
24316-8 Pa. **$9.95**

COMPLETE PRELUDES AND ETUDES FOR SOLO PIANO, Frédéric Chopin. All 26 Preludes, all 27 Etudes by greatest composer of piano music. Authoritative Paderewski edition. 224pp. 9 × 12. (Available in U.S. only)
24052-5 Pa. **$8.95**

COMPLETE BALLADES, IMPROMPTUS AND SONATAS, Frédéric Chopin. The four Ballades, four Impromptus and three Sonatas. Authoritative Paderewski edition. 240pp. 9 × 12. (Available in U.S. only)
24164-5 Pa. **$9.95**

NOCTURNES AND POLONAISES, Frédéric Chopin. 19 *Nocturnes* and 16 *Polonaises* reproduced from the authoritative Paderewski Edition for pianists, students, and musicologists. Commentary. viii + 272pp. 9 × 12. (Available in U.S. only)
24564-0 Pa. **$10.95**

COMPLETE MAZURKAS, Frédéric Chopin. 51 best-loved compositions, reproduced directly from the authoritative Kistner edition edited by Carl Mikuli. 160pp. 9 × 12.
25548-4 Pa. **$8.95**

FANTASY IN F MINOR, BARCAROLLE, BERCEUSE AND OTHER WORKS FOR SOLO PIANO, Frédéric Chopin. 15 works, including one of the greatest of the Romantic period, the Fantasy in F Minor, Op. 49, reprinted from the authoritative German edition prepared by Chopin's student, Carl Mikuli. 224pp. 8¾ × 11¼.
25950-1 Pa. **$7.95**

COMPLETE HUNGARIAN RHAPSODIES FOR SOLO PIANO, Franz Liszt. All 19 Rhapsodies reproduced directly from an authoritative Russian edition. All headings, footnotes translated to English. Best one volume edition available. 224pp. 8⅜ × 11¼.   24744-9 Pa. **$9.95**

ANNÉES DE PÈLERINAGE, COMPLETE, Franz Liszt. Authoritative Russian edition of piano masterpieces: *Première Année (Suisse): Deuxième Année (Italie)* and *Venezia e Napoli; Troisième Année*, other related pieces. 288pp. 9⅜ × 12¼.
25627-8 Pa. **$12.95**

COMPLETE ETUDES FOR SOLO PIANO, Series I: Including the Transcendental Etudes, Franz Liszt, edited by Busoni. Also includes Etude in 12 Exercises, 12 Grandes Etudes and Mazeppa. Breitkopf & Härtel edition. 272pp. 8⅜ × 11¼.
25815-7 Pa. **$11.95**

COMPLETE ETUDES FOR SOLO PIANO, Series II: Including the Paganini Etudes and Concert Etudes, Franz Liszt, edited by Busoni. Also includes Morceau de Salon, Ab Irato. Breitkopf & Härtel edition. 192pp. 8⅜ × 11¼.
25816-5 Pa. **$9.95**

SONATA IN B MINOR AND OTHER WORKS FOR PIANO, Franz Liszt. One of Liszt's most performed piano masterpieces, with the six Consolations, ten *Harmonies poetiques et religieuses*, two Ballades and two Legendes. Breitkopf and Härtel edition. 208pp. 8⅜ × 11¼.
26182-4 Pa. **$9.95**

PIANO TRANSCRIPTIONS FROM FRENCH AND ITALIAN OPERAS, Franz Liszt. Virtuoso transformations of themes by Mozart, Verdi, Bellini, other masters, into unforgettable music for piano. Published in association with American Liszt Society. 247pp. 9 × 12.
24273-0 Pa. **$12.95**

MEPHISTO WALTZ AND OTHER WORKS FOR SOLO PIANO, Franz Liszt. Rapsodie Espagnole, Liebestraüme Nos. 1-3, Valse Oubliée No. 1, Nuages Gris, Polonaises Nos. 1 and 2, Grand Galop Chromatique, more. 192pp. 8⅜ × 11¼.
28147-7 Pa. **$9.95**

COMPLETE WORKS FOR PIANOFORTE SOLO, Felix Mendelssohn. Breitkopf and Härtel edition of Capriccio in F# Minor, Sonata in E Major, Fantasy in F# Minor, Three Caprices, Songs without Words, and 20 other works. Total of 416pp. 9⅜ × 12¼. Two-vol. set.
23136-4, 23137-2 Pa. **$21.90**

COMPLETE SONATAS AND VARIATIONS FOR SOLO PIANO, Johannes Brahms. All sonatas, five variations on themes from Schumann, Paganini, Handel, etc. Vienna Gesellschaft der Musikfreunde edition. 178pp. 9 × 12.
22650-6 Pa. **$9.95**

COMPLETE SHORTER WORKS FOR SOLO PIANO, Johannes Brahms. All solo music not in other two volumes. Waltzes, Scherzo in E Flat Minor, Eight Pieces, Rhapsodies, Fantasies, Intermezzi, etc. Vienna Gesellschaft der Musikfreunde. 180pp. 9 × 12.
22651-4 Pa. **$9.95**

COMPLETE TRANSCRIPTIONS, CADENZAS AND EXERCISES FOR SOLO PIANO, Johannes Brahms. Vienna Gesellschaft der Musikfreunde edition, vol. 15. Studies after Chopin, Weber, Bach; gigues, sarabandes; 10 Hungarian dances, etc. 178pp. 9 × 12.
22652-2 Pa. **$10.95**

PIANO MUSIC OF ROBERT SCHUMANN, Series I, edited by Clara Schumann. Major compositions from the period 1830-39; *Papillons,* Toccata, Grosse Sonate No. 1, *Phantasiestücke, Arabeske, Blumenstück,* and nine other works. Reprinted from Breitkopf & Härtel edition. 274pp. 9⅜ × 12¼.
21459-1 Pa. **$12.95**

PIANO MUSIC OF ROBERT SCHUMANN, Series II, edited by Clara Schumann. Major compositions from period 1838-53; *Humoreske, Novelletten,* Sonate No. 2, 43 *Clavierstücke für die Jugend,* and six other works. Reprinted from Breitkopf & Härtel edition. 272pp. 9⅜ × 12¼.
21461-3 Pa. **$12.95**

PIANO MUSIC OF ROBERT SCHUMANN, Series III, edited by Clara Schumann. All solo music not in other two volumes, including *Symphonic Etudes, Phantaisie,* 13 other choice works. Definitive Breitkopf & Härtel edition. 224pp. 9⅜ × 12¼.
23906-3 Pa. **$10.95**

PIANO MUSIC 1888-1905, Claude Debussy. Deux Arabesques, Suite Bergamesque, Masques, first series of Images, etc. Nine others, in corrected editions. 175pp. 9⅜ × 12¼.
22771-5 Pa. **$7.95**

COMPLETE PRELUDES, Books 1 and 2, Claude Debussy. 24 evocative works that reveal the essence of Debussy's genius for musical imagery, among them many of the composer's most famous piano compositions. Glossary of French terms. 128pp. 8⅜ × 11¼.
25970-6 Pa. **$6.95**

PRELUDES, BOOK 1: The Autograph Score, Claude Debussy. Superb facsimile reproduced directly from priceless autograph score in Pierpont Morgan Library in New York. New Introduction by Roy Howat. 48pp. 8⅜ × 11.
25549-2 Pa. **$8.95**

PIANO MASTERPIECES OF MAURICE RAVEL, Maurice Ravel. Handsome affordable treasury; *Pavane pour une infante defunte, jeux d'eau, Sonatine, Miroirs,* more. 128pp. 9 × 12. (Not available in France or Germany)
25137-3 Pa. **$7.95**

COMPLETE LYRIC PIECES FOR PIANO, Edvard Grieg. All 66 pieces from Grieg's ten sets of little mood pictures for piano, favorites of generations of pianists. 224pp. 9⅜ × 12¼.
26176-X Pa. **$10.95**

*Available from your music dealer or write for **free** Music Catalog to*
Dover Publications, Inc., Dept. MUBI, 31 East 2nd Street, Mineola, N.Y. 11501.

Dover Popular Songbooks

"FOR ME AND MY GAL" AND OTHER FAVORITE SONG HITS, 1915–1917, David A. Jasen (ed.). 31 great hits: Pretty Baby, MacNamara's Band, Over There, Old Grey Mare, Beale Street, M-O-T-H-E-R, more, with original sheet music covers, complete vocal and piano. 144pp. 9 × 12. 28127-2 Pa. **$9.95**

POPULAR IRISH SONGS, Florence Leniston (ed.). 37 all-time favorites with vocal and piano arrangements: "My Wild Irish Rose," "Irish Eyes are Smiling," "Last Rose of Summer," "Danny Boy," many more. 160pp. 26755-5 Pa. **$9.95**

FAVORITE SONGS OF THE NINETIES, edited by Robert Fremont. 88 favorites: "Ta-Ra-Ra-Boom-De-Aye," "The Band Played on," "Bird in a Gilded Cage," etc. 401pp. 9 × 12. 21536-9 Pa. **$15.95**

POPULAR SONGS OF NINETEENTH-CENTURY AMERICA, edited by Richard Jackson. 64 most important songs: "Old Oaken Bucket," "Arkansas Traveler," "Yellow Rose of Texas," etc. 290pp. 9 × 12. 23270-0 Pa. **$12.95**

SONG HITS FROM THE TURN OF THE CENTURY, edited by Paul Charosh, Robert A. Fremont. 62 bit hits: "Silver Heels," "My Sweetheart's the Man in the Moon," etc. 296pp. 9 × 12. (Except British Commonwealth [but may be sold in Canada]) 23158-5 Pa. **$8.95**

ALEXANDER'S RAGTIME BAND AND OTHER FAVORITE SONG HITS, 1901–1911, edited by David A. Jasen. Fifty vintage popular songs America still sings, reprinted in their entirety from the original editions. Introduction. 224pp. 9 × 12. (Available in U.S. only) 25331-7 Pa. **$11.95**

"PEG O' MY HEART" AND OTHER FAVORITE SONG HITS, 1912 & 1913, edited by Stanley Appelbaum. 36 songs by Berlin, Herbert, Handy and others, with complete lyrics, full piano arrangements and original sheet music covers in black and white. 176pp. 9 × 12. 25998-6 Pa. **$12.95**

SONGS OF THE CIVIL WAR, Irwin Silber (ed.). Piano, vocal, guitar chords for 125 songs including *Battle Cry of Freedom, Marching Through Georgia, Dixie, Oh, I'm a Good Old Rebel, The Drummer Boy of Shiloh,* many more. 400pp. 8⅜ × 11. 28438-7 Pa. **$14.95**

AMERICAN BALLADS AND FOLK SONGS, John A. Lomax and Alan Lomax. Over 200 songs, music and lyrics: *Frankie and Albert, John Henry, Frog Went a-Courtin', Down in the Valley, Skip to My Lou,"* other favorites. Notes on each song. 672pp. 5⅜ × 8¼. 28276-7 Pa. **$12.95**

"TAKE ME OUT TO THE BALL GAME" AND OTHER FAVORITE SONG HITS, 1906–1908, edited by Lester Levy. 23 favorite songs from the turn-of-the-century with lyrics and original sheet music covers: "Cuddle Up a Little Closer, Lovey Mine," "Harrigan," "Shine on, Harvest Moon," "School Days," other hits. 128pp. 9 × 12. 24662-0 Pa. **$7.95**

THE AMERICAN SONG TREASURY: 100 Favorites, edited by Theodore Raph. Complete piano arrangements, guitar chords and lyrics for 100 best-loved tunes, "Buffalo Gals," "Oh, Suzanna," "Clementine," "Camptown Races," and much more. 416pp. 8⅜ × 11. 25222-1 Pa. **$14.95**

"THE ST. LOUIS BLUES" AND OTHER SONG HITS OF 1914, edited by Sandy Marrone. Full vocal and piano for "By the Beautiful Sea," "Play a Simple Melody," "They Didn't Believe Me," 21 songs in all. 112pp. 9 × 12. 26383-5 Pa. **$7.95**

STEPHEN FOSTER SONG BOOK, Stephen Foster. 40 favorites: "Beautiful Dreamer," "Camptown Races," "Jeanie with the Light Brown Hair," "My Old Kentucky Home," etc. 224pp. 9 × 12. 23048-1 Pa. **$8.95**

ONE HUNDRED ENGLISH FOLKSONGS, edited by Cecil J. Sharp. Border ballads, folksongs, collected from all over Great Britain. "Lord Bateman," "Henry Martin," "The Green Wedding," many others. Piano. 235pp. 9 × 12. 23192-5 Pa. **$13.95**

THE CIVIL WAR SONGBOOK, edited by Richard Crawford. 37 songs: "Battle Hymn of the Republic," "Drummer Boy of Shiloh," "Dixie," 33 more. 157pp. 9 × 12. 23422-3 Pa. **$8.95**

SONGS OF WORK AND PROTEST, Edith Fowke, Joe Glazer. 100 important songs: "Union Maid," "Joe Hill," "We Shall Not Be Moved," many more. 210pp. 7⅞ × 10¼. 22899-1 Pa. **$10.95**

A RUSSIAN SONG BOOK, edited by Rose N. Rubin and Michael Stillman. 25 traditional folk songs, plus 19 popular songs by twentieth-century composers. Full piano arrangements, guitar chords. Lyrics in original Cyrillic, transliteration and English translation. With discography. 112pp. 9 × 12. 26118-2 Pa. **$8.95**

FAVORITE CHRISTMAS CAROLS, selected and arranged by Charles J. F. Cofone. Title, music, first verse and refrain of 34 traditional carols in handsome calligraphy; also subsequent verses and other information in type. 79pp. 8⅜ × 11. 20445-6 Pa. **$4.95**

SEVENTY SCOTTISH SONGS, Helen Hopekirk (ed.). Complete piano and vocals for classics of Scottish song: *Flow Gently, Sweet Afton, Comin' thro' the Rye (Gin a Body Meet a Body), The Campbells are Comin', Robin Adair,* many more. 208pp. 8⅜ × 11. 27029-7 Pa. **$10.95**

   1. Books may be kept two weeks and may be
renewed twice for the same period, unless reserved.

   2. A fine is charged for each day a book is not
returned according to the above rule. No book will
be issued to any person incurring such a fine until it
has been paid.

   3. All injuries to books beyond reasonable wear
and all losses shall be made good to the satisfaction
of the Librarian.

   4. Each borrower is held responsible for all books
charged on his card and for all fines accruing on the
same.

GAYLORD

OVERSIZE